RISE Above AI Chaos

A Business Fable About Leading Organizations Through the AI Revolution

Floor Blindenbach

First Paperback Edition

The principles illustrated in this book are informed by methods developed through the work of Organizing4Innovation.

Published by Freiling Agency, LLC.

P.O. Box 1264

Warrenton, VA 20188

www.FreilingAgency.com

PB ISBN: 978-1-963701-96-8
E-book ISBN: 978-1-963701-97-5

For Wim

Contents

Introduction

This book isn't just a story about technology. It's about trust, ambition, and the messy reality of change.

Generative Artificial Intelligence (GenAI) is arguably the most powerful technology of our era, but in business, adoption is slow and failure rates are high. According to a recent MIT study, 95 percent of GenAI pilots don't deliver. Why? Not because the tech is broken, but because the real obstacles are cultural: unrealistic expectations, misaligned incentives, and mistrust.

Fixing these problems isn't as simple as just trying harder… That's why this business fable is for anyone looking to execute a successful AI strategy—and willing to try an alternative approach by viewing GenAI adoption as a journey.

It's about making GenAI work—not just as a tool, but as a catalyst for transformation.

Revolution?

GenAI is often hailed as the steam engine of our era—a force with the power to reshape industries, redefine white-collar work, and upend the value of expertise. But history teaches us that revolutions aren't triggered by technology alone.

When James Watt refined the steam engine in the eighteenth century, it was a breakthrough—an elegant solution that made steam power practical for industry. Its early impact was greatest in mines and mills, where it powered pumps and machinery and helped launch the Industrial Revolution. The real shift came when innovators like George Stephenson looked beyond stationary uses and imagined how steam might move people and goods. By embracing new high-pressure designs that Watt himself had resisted, they transformed the engine from an industrial workhorse into the force that powered locomotives and connected cities. As steam spread, mill owners harnessed it to drive looms and machinery, turning local crafts into global industries. The machine was the spark, but it was human ingenuity that built the railways, factories, and shipping lines that changed the world.

And yet, even as steam reshaped society, these new technologies continued to face old fears. When the first automobiles appeared decades later, Britain passed what became known as the Red Flag Act: a law requiring a person to walk ahead of every motor car, waving a flag or carrying a lantern to warn pedestrians. These first automobiles could have gone faster, farther, and opened entirely new possibilities—but instead they crawled behind a human pacesetter. It's a striking example of how innovation can be ready to transform the world, while our instincts for caution hold it back.

Today, GenAI sits at a similar crossroads. In boardrooms and breakrooms, leaders debate its promise. Some wait for the perfect roadmap; others experiment, stumble, and learn. The winners won't be those with the fanciest tech stack—they'll be the ones who let GenAI deliver its true potential rather than walking in front of it with a red flag, slowing it to the pace of old habits and old fears.

The future will belong to those who turn GenAI into a living, breathing part of the daily work—using it to solve real problems and create new, defensible value streams.

Standing at the threshold of this new era, the challenge is to move beyond GenAI—to imagine, adapt, and build new ways of working that previously were deemed impossible, and thereby multiplying GenAI's impact. This book is about that messy, creative, and sometimes uncomfortable process: making GenAI work, not just for your workflows, but for your organization's future.

Why a Story?

Most business books about AI transformation read like technical manuals—filled with frameworks, statistics, and step-by-step implementation guides. While these resources have their place, they often overlook the most critical element of organizational change: the complex, unpredictable, and deeply human reality of how people respond to new technology.

The truth is, GenAI adoption doesn't fail because of inadequate processing power or insufficient algorithms. It fails because of office politics, generational differences, and competing priorities—and because of an age-old tension between those who champion change and those who bear the burden of implementing it. Layered on top of that is the persistent pull to prioritize today's results and profits over tomorrow's.

These dynamics can't be captured in a flowchart or reduced to a checklist. They live in the spaces between meetings, in the unspoken frustrations that build over months, and in the small daily interactions that either build momentum or create resistance. A story allows us to explore these human elements in their full complexity, to see not just what people do, but why they do it.

By following the journey of five archetypal business characters through an AI transformation, this book examines the psychological and social forces that determine success or failure. The story addresses those moments when good intentions collide with practical constraints, when individual fears override organizational goals, and when small misunderstandings cascade into major obstacles.

This approach isn't just more engaging. It's more honest. Because when you strip away the jargon and the PowerPoint presentations, every AI transformation is ultimately a human story.

The Five Key Players

To make this book practical and to ensure the human aspects are properly addressed, it focuses on five key stakeholders who play crucial roles in adopting GenAI and embracing agentic workflows within any organization. These are the people you'll likely recognize in your own workplace:

- **Bailey the Boss:** Visionary CEO, caught between boardroom pressure and the reality of slow GenAI adoption.
- **Drew the Department Head:** Pragmatic leader, skeptical of change that doesn't make life easier for her team or clients.
- **Ira from IT:** The steady hand, always there to offer support for innovation, but feeling the squeeze of limited resources.
- **Taylor the Young Talent:** Ambitious associate, eager to prove herself but anxious about GenAI's impact on her future.
- **Van the Vendor:** Smooth-talking sales rep, selling dreams of transformation but focused on closing deals.

Bailey the Boss

Bailey is the CEO, the grand strategist, the fearless leader—or at least, that's how he likes to portray himself. He thrives on bold moves, big visions, and making sure the firm is always ahead of the competition. He trusts his instincts, loves big ideas, and despises getting bogged down in operational details. Luck played a big role in his successful career, but he'd never admit it.

Since last year, Bailey has been pushing hard for GenAI adoption. At first, he was highly skeptical, but now he is convinced it will revolutionize their industry. Over the past nine months, he has been pushing to make generic and specialized GenAI solutions available firm-wide in an effort to catch up. To his frustration, fewer than 40 percent of employees are currently using the expensive tools he championed. Now, he's caught between the pressure from the board to justify skyrocketing IT costs and his own gut feeling that AI is the future. If only he could get his people on board.

Drew the Department Head

Drew is the linchpin between leadership's grand vision and the messy reality of day-to-day operations. She earned her position through years of hard work, expertise, and sheer perseverance. A master of her craft, she knows exactly how things get done and how much effort every so-called "innovation" requires to get from idea to results.

She's seen technology fads come and go, and while she's open to change, she doesn't have the patience for disruptions that don't make life easier. GenAI? Maybe useful for automating emails and generating reports, but she's not convinced it's worth reworking everything she's spent years perfecting. Her main frustration is that someone like Bailey has no idea or appreciation for how much effort change really takes on her and her team.

Ira from IT (or Innovation)

Ira is the steady hand behind the firm's digital evolution—a quiet force who balances innovation with security and stability, cheerleading change and leading from behind. Throughout her career, she's navigated every major technological shift, from the dawn of personal computing to the rise of the cloud, and now, the tidal wave of AI.

She believes in GenAI's potential—but she also knows that most executives don't truly understand what they're asking for when they demand it.

Just a year ago, her focus was on blocking unauthorized use of GenAI tools. Now, Bailey is urging her to embed AI across every business function and operation. Ira is exhausted, overwhelmed, and increasingly wary of bold promises that gloss over the messy, resource-intensive reality of implementation. In the end, it is her team that needs to make all these projects happen.

She oversees the IT budget, but the board holds the purse strings. That leaves her constantly squeezed between sky-high expectations and constrained resources. The firm has spent a lot on GenAI tools, but if it had been up to her, she would have approached it differently, because, unsurprisingly, adoption challenges are mounting. What makes the current GenAI frenzy even more maddening is the assumption that by making (expensive) tools available, costs and time will be saved. In practice, it means she's being asked to deliver more, faster, with less.

Taylor the Young Talent

Taylor is an ambitious, restless associate who thrives on learning, moving fast, and making an impact. She's impatient, eager to prove herself, and completely comfortable using GenAI for everything—from home projects, to summarizing long-form content, to drafting client reports.

Her relationship with GenAI, however, is not uncomplicated. On one hand, she quietly worries that the same technology helping her excel could eventually make her role obsolete. On the other, she fears something far more immediate: getting stuck doing work that feels meaningless, repetitive, and disconnected from any real value. She grew up in a world of instant answers and has little patience for long meetings, hour-long training sessions, or outdated processes.

Taylor doesn't read manuals; she figures things out as she goes. She's willing to put in extra hours—if the work is engaging. If it's not? She's already looking for her next career move.

Van the Vendor

Van is a smooth-talking sales rep who sells AI solutions for a living. He's charming, persistent, and laser-focused on one thing: hitting his sales quota. Making clients happy is great, but closing deals is his top priority.

He knows that selling directly to Ira, the IT head, is tough. IT departments have strict budgets and long approval cycles. So instead, he is reaching out to old friends like Taylor and people he knew from his university days, like Drew. If he can get them excited, getting executive buy-in becomes much easier.

Van isn't just selling AI—he's selling dreams of efficiency, transformation, and competitive advantage. He genuinely believes in his product, but he also knows that 75 percent of the software he has sold will never make it past the pilot phase. That's not his problem, though—he's on to the next deal.

Bringing AI to Life in an Organization

None of these characters are real, but each is drawn from the lived reality of organizations wrestling with change. Their stories are inspired by the experiences of the author's clients: teams and leaders who have navigated the uncertainty, hope, and frustration of GenAI adoption; the visionaries who push for transformation; the skeptics who guard what works; the quiet hands who keep systems running; the restless talents eager to prove themselves; and the vendors who promise the future.

Their journey unfolds at Vic Titious LLP, a fictional firm with a legacy stretching back more than seventy-five years. Once a small consultancy, Vic Titious has grown into a professional services powerhouse—750 employees, $150 million in revenue, and a reputation for expertise. Yet, like so many established companies, it faces the relentless pressure to adapt because of new technologies, shifting client demands, and the ever-present risk of falling behind.

Vic Titious is a composite—part law firm, part engineering consultancy, part advisory practice. Its challenges are universal: legacy systems, siloed teams, and the tension between safeguarding today's profits and sustaining future revenues. As you read, imagine your own organization in its place. The names and details may change, but the dilemmas, ambitions, and breakthroughs are shared by every team trying to rise above the chaos of AI-driven change.

The Six Parts of This Book

This book is structured as a six-part transformation journey, guiding you through the process of successfully implementing AI-powered workflows:

1. **Chaos and Opportunity**
2. **Prioritizing Projects**
3. **Developing the Solution**
4. **Pivots and Unexpected Turns**
5. **Delivering Value and ROI**
6. **Conclusion: The Real Work Begins**

Let's start the journey…

"The hardest part of GenAI adoption isn't the tool. It's the trust."

PART 1
Chaos and Opportunity

Bailey's Dilemma: The View from the Top

Bailey stared at the quarterly reports, the numbers blurring as the knot in his stomach tightened. Competitors were racing ahead, announcing bold GenAI initiatives with fanfare. Vic Titious was late to the game, and despite his scramble to catch up, results had been elusive. The board's patience was thinning—and Bailey could feel it.

"We need big results with GenAI," the chairman had said, his tone leaving no room for debate. Bailey knew it wouldn't be easy.

Adopting GenAI had required a full 180-degree pivot from their original strategy. And yet, all things considered, that zigzag was the least of his worries.

The management team still had scars from their last major initiative—the firm's accounting system overhaul. While technically successful, it had taken more than three years to complete and drained time, energy, and goodwill. And then there was the sustainability initiative that topped the agenda just two years ago, that now sat in limbo, a silent monument to unrealized promises.

GenAI felt different though. Everything Bailey was reading—and hearing from his CEO peers—suggested that this was the next big leap. The technology promised huge efficiency gains and a significant elevation of work quality. But what would that actually look like in practice? Would it mean layoffs? Would it erode mentorship and hands-on training for younger staff? And where would the growth come from?

And more urgently: Where would they find the time, energy, and money to take on such a transformation initiative?

Bailey replayed a moment from a recent management meeting, the tension still fresh in his mind.

Ira had been animated, leaning forward in her chair as she spoke. "Look, I know we've had mixed results with the Microsoft Copilot rollout, but agentic workflows are different. Think of them as smart assistants that can complete tasks. They could automate our client intake process, generate initial risk assessments, even draft contract summaries."

Her eyes had brightened as she warmed to the topic. "Imagine if onboarding a new client took hours instead of days. Suppose our junior associates could focus on analysis instead of data entry. What if we could give clients preliminary insights within 24 hours of their first call?"

Bailey remembered how the energy in the room had shifted. A few heads nodding. People sat up straighter.

Then Drew had spoken.

"Ira, I appreciate the enthusiasm, really." Her tone had been measured, professional, but firm. "But we don't have the bandwidth to experiment with shiny new tools right now. My team is already stretched thin trying to meet Q3 targets."

"This isn't just experimentation—" Ira had started.

"It is, though." Drew had cut her off, not unkindly but decisively. "Every new system means training time. Learning curves. Debugging issues. My people are working 50-plus-hour weeks as it is. They need to stay focused on hitting revenue targets—period."

The room had gone quiet. Bailey could still picture Ira's face—the way her excitement had deflated, replaced by that familiar look of someone whose vision had just hit a wall of operational reality.

"Besides," Drew had continued, her voice softer now, "what happens when GenAI makes a mistake? When it misses a crucial detail in a contract or gives a client bad advice? My name is on those deliverables. My relationships are on the line."

That exchange had stuck with Bailey. Because, frustratingly, they were both right.

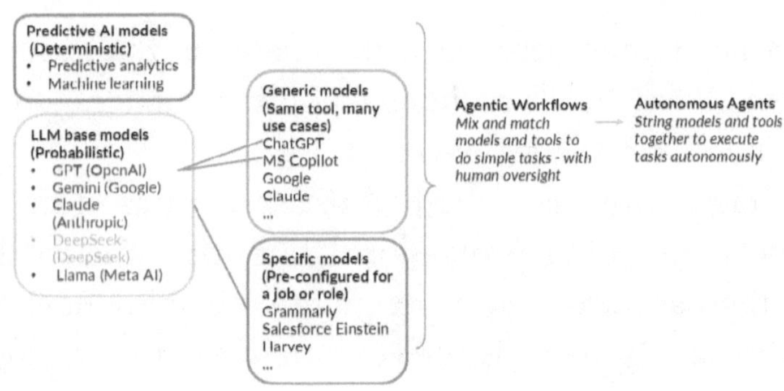

Figure 1: Agentic Workflows: The Middle Ground Between Predictive AI and Autonomous Agents

Bailey picked up the printout Ira had left behind—the slide with boxes and arrows mapping this strange new AI universe. He studied it again. At the top: traditional predictive models, the part he understood. At the bottom: Large Language Models, the engines behind tools like Microsoft Copilot—the technology the firm had just adopted. And in the middle, a phrase that still felt abstract:

Agentic workflows.

He could hear Ira's voice from the meeting, clear and insistent:

"These aren't just bots," she had said, tapping the diagram. *"Predictive AI follows rules—leading to deterministic outcomes. GenAI creates options—predictions derived from previous information. Agentic workflows combine these technologies—automating tasks using deterministic and probabilistic AI, with human oversight."*

He wanted to believe Ira when she said the technology was ready. But he'd been around long enough to know that tech alone never solves anything. And it seemed he wasn't alone—while many of the competitors were making big claims online, he knew from private conversations that most were struggling to turn GenAI's promises into measurable progress. An MBA classmate had shared that he had provided LawBot—a legal-industry AI platform for research and drafting—to everyone in his firm. It had been a huge investment, but fewer than half their people were using the tool. Vic Titious seemed to be no different, but fortunately, they had not shouted their more modest investments from the rooftops. As Ira had warned him, it is one thing to give everyone access to GenAI tools—but quite another to generate a return from that investment and grow revenues.

What kept him up at night wasn't the software. It was the people.

How could he get Drew's already overloaded department to adopt new ways of working that would help them save time? How could he help Ira bridge the gap between IT's capabilities and what the business actually needed? And how could he support both of them without burning them—or himself—out?

Was announcing a bold, firm-wide initiative the right move, as the chairman had urged?

"Go big or go home"—was that the answer?

Maybe. A big initiative certainly could put Vic

Titious on the map. But what would "big" even look like? Giving a tool like LawBot to everyone in the firm was no longer a move that would make headlines.

What Are Agentic Workflows?

To understand agentic workflows, it helps to first distinguish them from other ways AI is commonly used in organizations.

- Generative AI on its own is typically used as a tool—something people prompt to draft text, summarize information, or answer questions. It's powerful for individuals, but disconnected from broader workflows.
- Predictive AI and traditional automation rely on predefined rules and stable data. They work well for repeatable tasks, but struggle when conditions change or judgment is required.
- Fully autonomous agents take action on their own, with minimal human involvement. While promising, they raise concerns around trust, safety, and accountability—especially in professional services.

Agentic workflows sit deliberately in between. They use GenAI's ability to interpret context, generate options, and adapt to new information—while keeping humans in control at critical decision points.

Rather than replacing people or handing over full autonomy, agentic workflows are designed to *support* complex work that involves judgment, trade-offs, and responsibility.

Key Features

- **Blended Intelligence**
  Agentic workflows use GenAI to handle complexity and speed up work, while people stay in control of decisions and outcomes.
- **Oversight by Design**
  Human review and accountability are built into the workflow itself, rather than added later as a safeguard.
- **Flexible by Nature**
  These workflows can grow and adapt over time, keeping pace with changing needs, tools, and ways of working.

Drew's Challenge: Driving Today's and Tomorrow's Revenues

Drew had been running the Corporate Department at Vic Titious for seven years. She knew every process, every bottleneck, and every workaround her team had ever developed. So when Bailey first mentioned the firm's AI transformation, her gut reaction was immediate:

"Great. Another initiative that's going to distract us

from the real work."

Drew wasn't convinced GenAI was the solution—or even the right path forward at this moment. She was wary of even more "Big Brother" oversight by AI. Some days, she would think twice before going to the bathroom or getting a second cup of coffee, as it would negatively impact her billable-hour targets. *Please,* she thought, *don't introduce yet another system watching over my shoulder while I am trying to earn money for the firm.*

But what frustrated her even more was the silence around the firm's sustainability initiative—*her* initiative. She had championed it. Led the early efforts. Scored a few wins. Then… life got in the way. Deadlines. Clients. Staffing. The kind of everyday pressures that slowly chip away at even the most promising change efforts. Still, Drew wasn't ready to let it go. To her, it was the right thing to do, but she understood the timing was currently far from optimal, as sustainability had slipped down the priority list for many of their clients. Nevertheless, she'd rather finish what they had started than chase the next shiny object. What also worried her was that GenAI might actively undermine the progress they'd made.

GenAI, from what she'd read, came with a steep energy bill. Vic Titious had made a public pledge to run on sustainable energy—back then, an easy promise for a professional service firm. But if Bailey and the leadership team started seeing rising server costs, would they walk that back? *All that good PR, all that investment in our values—gone,* she feared. *And for what? Some tech that delivers unpredictable results.*

From where she stood, GenAI looked overhyped. Powerful, maybe. But immature. As a colleague had explained to her, "GenAI is like hiring an intern who could do great work—but only with constant supervision." She also worried about the expertise the firm had built up over the years—how would that stack up against a bot with an insatiable appetite to devour data?

She had tried ChatGPT at home, and while it had provided a few helpful results, when she had asked it questions related to her work, the results felt flat, too simple, and unimpressive. *Let someone else babysit the bot this time,* she thought. *My team has done enough.*

Still, there was Taylor. A quick study. Ambitious. Always looking for ways to do things faster or smarter. Drew found herself thinking back to one evening about a year ago, when GenAI was still strictly off-limits. Most of the team had already packed up for the night when Taylor lingered by the door, hovering in the way people do when they want to say something but aren't sure they should.

"Drew, can I talk to you about something?" she'd asked quietly. Drew remembered the way Taylor had glanced around the empty conference room, as if the walls might be listening.

She'd confessed, almost in a single breath, that she'd been *experimenting*—her word—with ChatGPT to draft client emails. Her hands had moved nervously as she explained that it cut her drafting time in half and, embarrassingly, made her emails sound better.

Drew remembered her own eyebrows lifting despite herself. "Better? How?" she'd asked, and Taylor had launched into an earnest explanation—how the tool helped her tighten her writing and avoid her usual rambling. She had been quick to insist she still reviewed everything, that she wasn't copying and pasting blindly.

At the time, Drew had felt herself start to object, and Taylor had immediately tensed, shoulders pulling up like she expected reprimand. Drew had stopped herself, told Taylor she wasn't criticizing—just processing. They'd stood in an awkward quiet for a moment, Drew watching that mix of guilt and excitement cross Taylor's face. She recognized it. Years ago, she had been in a similar position when she secretly used the first online databases before they had been officially approved.

On impulse, Drew had asked to see one of the emails. She could still picture Taylor's hesitation, before unlocking her phone and placing it carefully in Drew's hand. Drew remembered reading the "before" version—competent but wordy—and then the "after" produced by ChatGPT. Cleaner. More direct. Still sounding like Taylor, just a sharper version of her. That was the part that had unsettled Drew the most: that it still felt authentic.

Taylor had asked, almost in a whisper, whether Drew was going to report her. Drew remembered the young woman's fear, how vulnerable she suddenly seemed. She'd told her no—and urged Taylor to be careful. Drafting emails was one thing. Client analyses, legal reasoning, or strategic recommendations were something else entirely.

"Without approval? Without understanding the risks?" she had asked Taylor. "What happens when you get comfortable with the shortcut and it gives you something that sounds right but isn't? What happens when your own writing muscles weaken because the machine feels faster?" Taylor had admitted she hadn't thought about that.

Drew wasn't against innovation. She never was. She just had wanted Taylor to understand the trade-offs. GenAI had been deemed too risky to use by Vic Titious' leadership, and their guidelines could not be simply ignored.

And even now, months after the use of GenAI had been officially permitted, Drew was still conflicted. Taylor's communication skills had improved. But recently, she had wondered about an email that came from Taylor and if it had been written by GenAI. It sounded so formulaic. If Drew could pick that up—what would their clients think?

What's more, she didn't know how much time Taylor had spent on learning GenAI, crafting prompts, or double-checking results. And Drew had seen all too often that what looked like a shortcut typically came with hidden costs.

Besides, they had real work to do. Real deadlines. Real clients.

Experimentation is fine, Drew thought, *but not on company time. Not when the margins are already this tight.*

She trusted Taylor's intentions. But she also knew what could happen if just one AI-generated message went sideways. The headlines in the news were there—a mistake would easily be made. She could already see others on the team following Taylor's lead without oversight or guardrails—a nightmare scenario—because in the end, Drew would be on the hook if something went wrong.

She wasn't against new technology. She just knew what it took to make change stick. And this? A technology that didn't even claim to work perfectly. It was shaping up to be another time-sucking project with unclear payoff.

Ira's Frustration: The Technology–Reality Gap

Ira had been championing GenAI since the early days. She'd researched vendors, attended conferences, and decided that Microsoft Copilot—while far from perfect—would be a great starting point for the firm. She saw enormous potential—and even more pressure to get it right.

Turning enthusiasm into adoption—that felt like pushing a boulder uphill.

Her biggest challenge wasn't the tech. She knew what GenAI could do, but she didn't know enough about the day-to-day workflows in departments like Drew's to make it stick. There was always a gap between what was technically possible and what was practically useful.

Sure, summarizing emails or generating text drafts was

an easy win for everyone. But was that enough to justify the $300K Copilot rollout that Bailey had approved? Not likely.

Ira knew GenAI's real value wasn't in the tools—it was in rebuilding workflows so the firm could take advantage of the technology and its proprietary data. But creating such agentic workflows, that was a whole different ball game, one that demanded far more than anyone outside her team seemed to grasp.

Sure, there was the cost of the tools and the predictable headaches: the hours that went into testing, the meetings that spawned more meetings, the inevitable delays. And then the feature requests—always framed as tiny, harmless tweaks. "Just one more thing," their finance director had said more than once during the Accounting System Overhaul, unaware that those four words were the gateway to scope creep, blown timelines and budget overruns that ended up nearly killing the whole endeavor.

But what really exhausted Ira wasn't the work itself. It was the invisible work—the stuff nobody acknowledged but everyone relied on her to make happen.

There was the emotional babysitting of stakeholders who didn't know what they wanted yet still managed to be demanding. The rework caused by fuzzy expectations. The cybersecurity and governance tasks nobody liked, but their insurance company demanded. As a result, everyone assumed the appropriate checks would be put in place, even though no one took the time to make that happen. Instead, they tried to conveniently forget governance and cyber risks even existed.

And those were all small issues, compared to the really time-consuming stuff, such as documentation and training. Documentation was not a nice-to-have for Ira and her team. It took a lot of discipline to ensure all processes were properly documented, so that when people in her team came and went, the whole knowledge base would not evaporate. It was difficult enough to make her team document everything. But trying to convince anyone else outside IT that it mattered and should be budgeted for—Ira had found that to be a lost cause, which meant Ira's team paid for that neglect ten times over.

And then at the other end of this spectrum was training. Something that impacted everyone but never got the appropriate budget either. As a result, training workshops often amounted to a hastily stitched-together PowerPoint presentation, prepared the night before by someone from her team. And it would be Ira, who would have to field the complaints about the mandatory training.

Ira could feel her jaw tightening just thinking about it. Everyone wanted transformation, but nobody wanted to fund the parts that made transformation stick. *You want to know why most tech projects fail?* she thought. *Because we fund the software, not the system it takes to make it work.*

Ironically, if I added all those hours to the budget, nothing would ever get approved, Ira thought.

Worse. That invisibility made it even harder to build a case for the support systems needed to succeed.

And while leadership was finally on board to use GenAI firmwide, their expectations were... confusing. Less than a year ago, Bailey had asked Ira's team to block GenAI tool access. That decision led to frustration across the firm, and predictably, it drove employees to use tools like ChatGPT on personal devices. Now that Bailey had reversed course and provided Copilot licenses for the entire firm, everyone was scrambling—and Ira was left to clean up the mess.

Bailey wanted a big, bold initiative. Ira wanted a quick win. Something small but strategic—to rally the crowd and get more champions. But Bailey kept pushing her to think bigger and bolder. That made it harder to work on and deliver something small and real.

She considered pulling Drew in. They had worked well together during the Accounting System Overhaul. But lately, Drew had been less responsive. Ira suspected she was burned out and laser-focused on hitting her revenue targets.

Maybe I could build something for her without involving her team, Ira mused. But she knew how that story ended: with a solution that didn't fit, didn't scale, and didn't get used.

Another worry sat in the back of Ira's mind: data. Yes, with the new accounting system, IT had helped set up the new data infrastructure. But in practice? Only employees who had joined in the last three years followed the new guidelines. The old guard still relied on private folders—or worse, physical files. There was no single source of truth.

We're not ready for a big AI initiative, Ira thought. We're barely ready for standardized file-naming conventions.

Who Gets Involved (and Who Gets Burned Out)

Ira knew she couldn't deliver agentic workflows alone. She needed business input. But she was stuck in a loop.

Drew's team had always been her go-to for testing. They understood the importance of collaboration, gave thoughtful feedback, and delivered. But they were also overworked—and increasingly unavailable.

The Accounting System Overhaul had been a turning point. Its botched implementation had hurt her credibility. Even now, Ira's team was still fielding complaints.

"I can't keep going back to the same people for these projects," Ira realized. "It's not fair—and it's not scalable."

She needed new voices. New perspectives. But where to find them? She had influence, not authority. She couldn't just pull people from the departments. Her influence had limits—and the same volunteers were burning out.

Ira thought back to a principle she'd picked up from a conference: Stop relying on the willing few. It made her wonder, who stood to gain the most from GenAI? Who was drowning in manual work, desperate for relief? Who had been tinkering with GenAI under the radar, curious but unsupported?

Taylor immediately came to mind. She was one of the few GenAI users in Drew's group. If Ira could align the project goals with Taylor's daily struggles, she wouldn't just get participation. She might even get real buy-in.

To ensure she wouldn't burn out Taylor too, Ira planned to track every hour spent on the project. Leadership needed to see the hidden cost of innovation.

She leaned back, a flicker of hope replacing fatigue. Maybe the next wave wouldn't break the same people. Maybe it could lift everyone.

Taylor's Opportunity: Her Future Calling

When Taylor joined Vic Titious, four years ago now, she brought more than a fresh diploma and youthful energy—she brought ambition. Her colleagues saw her as "the tech-savvy young one," but what really drove her was a desire to make an impact. She wanted her work to matter.

So when she discovered GenAI, it felt like she'd found a secret weapon. Quietly, she began experimenting—using GenAI to draft responses, summarize lengthy documents, and streamline tedious tasks. It wasn't just about speed; the quality often improved, too. And best of all, it freed her up to focus on higher-value work.

Then came the new policy and the block on all GenAI use. That hit her hard. She started browsing job boards that same week. But after a few disappointing interviews and sometimes fierce competition from 100+ applicants, she decided to stay. There was still hope, she figured. Maybe she could find a way to prove AI's value from the inside.

She had been very glad when the firm made a 180-degree switch on the use of GenAI, but she still felt that there were more GenAI skeptics in the firm than enthusiasts. For example, recently she tried sharing one small win with Drew. The reaction was… underwhelming.

"Drew, I wanted to circle back on something," Taylor had begun, fidgeting with her pen. "I know ChatGPT isn't one of the preferred tools, and I know you have concerns, but it really helps me keep up with the workload. My turnaround times have improved by—"

"Taylor." Drew had looked up from her notes, her expression neutral but not unkind. "I appreciate that you're finding ways to be more efficient."

Taylor had leaned forward slightly, sensing an opening. "So maybe we could—"

"But right now," Drew continued, "I need to focus on the fundamentals. Speaking of keeping up, let's talk about your billable hours for this month. You're tracking at 129 hours, and we need you closer to 140 to hit our quarterly targets."

Taylor's shoulders had sagged almost imperceptibly. "Of course. The Henderson matter has been…"

"Good. Let's review your time entries and see where we can optimize."

And just like that, the conversation had moved to revenue targets. Client codes. Billing efficiency.

Taylor had gotten the message loud and clear: innovation could wait. Results couldn't. Better to run the long, familiar route than try a new, uncertain shortcut.

After that, Taylor kept her experiments under wraps. With a nudge from her friend Van (who always seemed to have a workaround), she found new ways to test tools on the side. But she didn't dare bring them up again. Drew was a solid manager, but when it came to AI, her focus was on compliance and deliverables—not exploration.

Then, there was the incident with IT. Taylor had accessed ChatGPT from her work laptop and received a follow-up email reminding her of the policy, that ChatGPT was not one of the approved tools. That confirmed it: she was being watched, and the risk of getting labeled a "rule breaker" felt too high.

So she waited.

Watched.

Quietly learning more and thinking of ways to improve her work while making sure nobody noticed she was using AI.

It wasn't that Taylor didn't want to help the firm—it was that she wasn't sure it would help her if she told anyone else. GenAI might be the future, but it could also jeopardize her present. Why take the risk?

Frontline Innovation

Taylor's story isn't unique. She's one of many frontline talented professionals who see opportunities long before leadership does. But until someone like Drew or Bailey signals support—until there's a clear path, safety net, and recognition—she will likely play it safe.

And that hesitation isn't just a missed opportunity for Taylor; it's a missed opportunity for Vic Titious.

It may help to know that many of history's greatest innovations didn't come from formal R&D departments—they came from people like Taylor. Gutenberg invented the printing press while trying to speed up his work. James Watt improved the steam engine while repairing it. Semmelweis realized the value of handwashing by observing daily hospital practices. They all changed the course of history with their discoveries.

Semmelweis's story is particularly telling. A junior doctor in 19th-century Vienna, he discovered that handwashing dramatically reduced maternal deaths. But because of his status—and because he challenged senior physicians—his insight was ignored. It wasn't until years later, through the work of Pasteur and Lister, that his findings were accepted.

The lesson? Transformative ideas often come from the frontline. But without sponsorship from above, they rarely break through.

For Taylor, return on investment isn't a number in the business case—it's a personal calculation. Her days are packed. She's expected to hit performance goals, respond to clients' questions, and keep up with training. That's her job.

Now add GenAI experimentation on top of all that. She could use her time at work to test tools that are not officially sanctioned—and risk missing her billable hour targets. Alternatively, she could use her personal time for things that should count as work. While Taylor valued her time, it wasn't even her biggest concern. She mostly wondered if she would be recognized if she succeeded—or reprimanded. And if she failed, would she be forgiven—or sidelined? For Taylor to step forward, the potential gain had to outweigh the risk. And as of now, that math didn't add up.

The ROI Dilemma: Why Results Matter and Numbers Aren't Enough

Like most organizations, Return on Investment (ROI) is the metric that gets innovation projects approved within Vic Titious. It's the number that signals ambition, justifies risk, and promises future value. Yet, once the business case is signed off on, something curious happens: the ROI target is quietly filed away.

No one wants to be held accountable for that number. Bailey and the board, who approved the investment, are not held accountable for delivering the results. The project team inherits this responsibility and the work, but they never made these promises. As conditions shift and priorities evolve, the original ROI becomes a distant memory—conveniently ignored when reality doesn't match projections.

And yet, ROI is the only yardstick Vic Titious has to evaluate whether a project like the Accounting System Overhaul delivered on its promise. With the results falling short, it became quickly clear that there was no clear owner of the gap and everyone knew what would happen next. Nothing.

To deliver on any investment made in GenAI, it is clear that Vic Titious needs more than a number in a business case. Bailey needs a way to make ROI a living commitment—one that is owned, supported, and revisited throughout the project's journey.

This is where the RISE framework comes in.

The RISE Framework

Since investment decisions are made at the top and innovation work unfolds at the front line, accountability for future returns dissolves somewhere in between.

In firms like Vic Titious, with no separate R&D unit that owns future value creation, innovation work competes with billable work, and outcomes benefit the collective more than the individual. As a result, participation in innovation projects becomes optional, returns feel distant, and accountability remains diffuse.

The RISE framework, developed through the work of Organizing4Innovation, is introduced here as a way of making these dynamics explicit—and of reconnecting investment decisions to the conditions that determine whether people commit and results materialize.

It consists of four dimensions—Return, Invest,

Support, and Expectations—that shape a person's willingness to commit to participating in an innovation effort and to delivering the expected returns.

Return

- What results are targeted?
- How is success recognized?
- Is there a safety net if things don't go as planned?

Invest

- Is this a real growth opportunity?
- Are there meaningful incentives to participate?
- Is this a rare opportunity—or just one of many?

Support

- Are there dedicated time and resources?
- Is there an offer for training or guidance?
- Will the team get timely feedback?

Expectations

- What's expected in terms of time and effort?
- Are participants asked to document and reflect on what they learn?
- Who gets credit—or blame—when the dust settles?

The RISE framework brings clarity to these conditions, ensuring that commitments are explicit and that the support needed to deliver results is in place.

The RISE Framework in Practice

The true power of the RISE framework as an alternative to traditional ROI calculations emerges when it's applied to real situations. In practice, RISE provides a lens to diagnose why people hesitate, what's missing from a project, and how to rebalance the conditions for success. By making these factors explicit, Vic Titious can turn potential into participation, and good intentions into measurable results.

For example, the RISE framework helps explain why Taylor hesitates. She sees the opportunity and the project genuinely interests her. But from her perspective, the equation doesn't yet add up.

For Taylor:

- **Return:** She might get recognition… or she might get nothing. There's no guarantee for a reward—or protection—if the project fails.
- **Invest:** It's a growth opportunity, yes. But she's expected to do it in her personal time. The incentives are unclear.
- **Support:** No time has been carved out. No training. At best, Taylor has a vague promise that Ira might help if things escalate.
- **Expectations:** No one has defined what success looks like, how much time the work will require, or how her performance will be evaluated.

Given these conditions, hesitation is not only understandable—it is the rational response.

A similar pattern appears for Drew.

For Drew:

- **Return:** The potential upside is real—greater efficiency could improve outcomes and even bonuses. But this gain is marginal compared to her broader responsibilities, and any misstep could jeopardize the reputation she has worked hard to build.
- **Invest:** Drew is at the peak of her career, with little left to prove. Unless the project aligns directly with her goals or positions her for a more strategic role, there is limited incentive to devote time to it.
- **Support:** Any additional work will fall on her already stretched team. There is no extra budget or buffer. She does, however, have a strong network she can rely on for feedback. Delegation is possible, but she will still need to oversee and champion the effort.
- **Expectations:** Managing the project, documenting progress, and capturing lessons along the way add yet another time demand she is not sure she can accommodate.

Why RISE Matters

The RISE framework highlights not only whether a project is worth pursuing, but whether the conditions exist for individuals to step up and make it work. When those conditions are missing—or when individual incentives are misaligned—the answer isn't to push harder. It's to rebalance the equation.

Give Taylor time, guidance, feedback, and recognition, and she probably will lean in. Show Drew how the project connects to her goals, and she might make room for it. Make expectations clear for both of them, and they will know what success looks like and what is required from them to reach the desired outcomes.

Rather than treating ROI as a distant metric or a forgotten promise, within RISE it serves as a living, collective commitment—one that aligns teams, drives accountability, and keeps the project's purpose front and center.

The New Reality: From Chaos to Commitment

The office had quieted down, but Bailey was still there. The city lights flickering against the glass behind him. The quarterly report pages were now spread across his desk, but his mind was elsewhere—on GenAI, on the board's pressure, and on the quiet hesitations he'd seen in that management meeting.

He thought about the Accounting System Overhaul—the scars it left, the fatigue it created. And now, here he was, contemplating something even bigger. GenAI wasn't just another system upgrade. It was a shift in how work happened, who did it, and what it meant to be an expert.

The promise was undeniable. Tools that could draft, summarize, analyze—tasks that once demanded hours of human effort, could now be completed in seconds. But promise alone didn't move people. He saw it in Drew's guarded tone, in Ira's frustration, in Taylor's silence. Everyone was circling the same question: *Is it worth the effort and the risk?*

And they weren't wrong to ask. Bailey was well aware that within Vic Titious, stepping forward often came at a cost. Extra hours. Extra scrutiny. Sometimes, even career risk. For Taylor, the calculation was personal: experiment on company time and risk reprimand—or do it after hours and hope someone would notice. For Drew, the stakes were higher still. Her reputation, her team's performance, her hard-won credibility—all on the line if GenAI stumbled.

Bailey understood their hesitation. GenAI didn't just change workflows; it challenged identities. Expertise that once took years to build could now be mimicked in seconds. That reality was unsettling—even for him. If the firm's value rested on knowledge, what would happen when knowledge became a commodity?

He leaned back, staring at Ira's slide which he had pinned to his wall: *An Agentic Workflow won't replace people—it changes what they're capable of.* He wanted to believe that. But he realized that the hardest part of GenAI adoption wasn't the tool. It was the trust. Trust that the outputs were reliable. Trust that mistakes wouldn't end careers. Trust that the effort would be recognized, not punished.

No one talked about that cultural shift out loud. It was on him to make that happen. Which made Bailey realize that the real cost of AI wasn't financial—it was operational and emotional. Without clarity and support, even the most promising initiative could feel like just another distraction—or worse, a threat.

Bailey tapped his pen against the desk, thinking about the big bang the board expected from him. A small investment with the promise of a big return—that is what the board expected. Bold numbers got projects approved. Yet, he had seen firsthand where that led to with the accounting project. He certainly didn't want to go down that path again.

Bailey closed his notebook slowly. GenAI wasn't just a technology shift. It was a leadership test. A trust test. And trust, Bailey knew, was harder to engineer than any workflow.

If Vic Titious could get this right—if they could move from chaos and curiosity to real commitment—they wouldn't just catch up. They'd pull ahead. The late founder of the firm, Vic Titious, would be proud. But bridges don't build themselves. Someone had to lead the way.

Bailey wondered if that someone was still him.

Part 1 Summary

Agentic workflows aren't just about faster outcomes; they're about smarter ways to deliver the same or better results.

Tailored offerings are Vic Titious' greatest asset—but unlocking this value with GenAI depends on creating an environment where professionals feel empowered and supported to design and implement new, agentic workflows that amplify their expertise and drive greater impact.

The RISE Framework helps uncover why people hesitate and what it takes to turn return on investment from a number into a commitment.

Key Takeaway

Leadership isn't about pushing harder—it's about creating the conditions where others want to contribute.

Reflection Questions

1. How is GenAI currently being used within your organization?
2. What are the most visible vs. invisible costs of experimenting with agentic workflows?
3. How does the RISE framework reflect your own experience with past projects?
4. What would success look like in your organization if a team got agentic workflows right?

What Kind of Contributor Are You?

If You're a Bailey (Executive Sponsor)

- Are you creating space—or pressure—for innovation?
- What obstacles can you remove, and what expectations are you setting?
- How often do you revisit the promises made in business cases?

If You're a Drew (Team Leader)

- Who are your "Taylors," and are you giving them room to try?
- Which unfinished initiatives are still worth pursuing—and which ones should be reconsidered?
- Could a small experiment with GenAI help explore how to make life easier for your team?

If You're an Ira (Innovation/IT Leader)

- Are you engaging the business or pushing from the sidelines?
- How are you building GenAI capabilities within departments like Drew's?
- Are your pilots designed for speed and stakeholder buy-in?

If You're a Taylor (Emerging Talent)

- Are you waiting for permission—or already experimenting?
- Do you understand the business enough to align your ideas?
- Who could help you turn a good hack into a real opportunity?

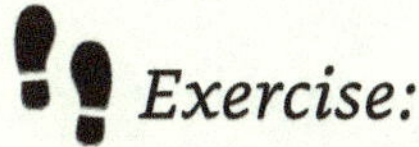

Exercise:

Mapping Commitment with the RISE Framework

Use the RISE model to assess your team's (or your own) readiness to engage with agentic workflows. Score the clarity you have on each component from 1–5 to identify imbalances or issues that may block progress.

Return

- What are the expected results?
- How will success be recognized?
- Is there a safety net for failure?

Invest

- Is this a meaningful growth opportunity?
- What are the incentives to participate?
- How rare or frequent is this kind of opportunity?

Support

- Is time allocated for this work?
- Are resources or training available?
- Is feedback from others easy to obtain?

Expectations

- Are the time commitment and responsibilities clearly defined?
- Is progress tracked and learning captured?
- Is attribution fair and transparent?

Add up your score and use that as a snapshot to identify who's ready to lead—and which areas or who needs more clarity, support, or incentive to join in.

"If an easy button existed, she would have found and pressed it a long time ago."

Part 2
Prioritizing Projects

Bailey's Lightbulb Moment

Bailey wasn't the kind of person to dwell on problems. He believed in action—find a solution, then move on.

So, when Bailey heard more about the concept of agentic workflows at a leadership conference, it wasn't the theory that grabbed him. It was a single phrase the speaker used: "Imagine if change happened automatically at the local level, without waiting for top-down approval."

That insight hit Bailey like a jolt. Because, unfortunately, new initiatives—whether adopting GenAI tools, improving knowledge management, launching the sustainability project, or updating templates—everything crawled along at a snail's pace at Vic Titious. Endless meetings, shifting priorities, and somehow, few things ever changed, or it took years—like the accounting project.

Now, armed with these new insights about agentic

workflows, he could picture internal projects moving forward because the people doing the work would have the tools and autonomy to act right away, without waiting for multiple levels of approval or for the IT department to make it all happen.

He imagined teams experimenting, adjusting, improving—all with just enough structure to stay aligned but without the drag of centralized control. It wasn't that Ira's team was hindering innovation—quite the opposite. But because everything had to go through them and all the departments kind of demanded that IT take the lead, the result was a bottleneck.

Before even discussing it with Ira or anyone else, he didn't just share the idea with clients—he promised it, casually dropping it into client conversations before anyone at the firm had even heard of his plans: "We're building a new way of working internally—one where change doesn't have to be managed top-down anymore. And you will continuously see better services and offerings from us—because our system will keep improving itself."

And that's when Bailey got carried away. He was selling a vision of a firm where internal excellence wasn't something they talked about, it was something they lived. That version of Vic Titious, however, was far from the current reality.

The Difference Bailey Wished into Existence

For Bailey the Sustainability initiative was the clearest example of what was amiss. Drew had spent months trying to kick off the sustainability program at Vic Titious.

The idea had sounded great in management meetings—reduce paper use, switch to energy-efficient lighting, recycle more, and encourage greener commuting options. Everyone had agreed it was important. Drew had put together a committee. They had surveyed employees. The sustainability committee had written a 30-page strategic plan. Then—and Bailey knew he was partly to blame—the report had sat on his desk for weeks. Momentum fizzled and six months later, the "Green Vic Titious" project was buried under more urgent priorities. In the end, nothing really changed. The firm still printed everything and recycled little.

The Difference: Sustainability Initiative

Before Agentic Workflows	With Agentic Workflows
A big sustainability plan was drafted by a committee	Small experiments launched by local teams
Long approval cycles, slow decision-making	Immediate action at the team level
No visible impact after six months	Quick wins create visible momentum

Sustainability seen as "extra work"	Sustainability becomes part of daily work
Energy fizzled out	Energy builds naturally

Why Bailey Got So Excited

For the first time in months, Bailey felt a spark—this wasn't just another initiative. It was a way to break free from the gridlock that had been suffocating Vic Titious. If they could make something as broad and fuzzy as *sustainability* move forward locally—just by empowering teams—they could apply the same approach to any stalled internal initiative: knowledge management, tech adoption, even client service innovations.

It wasn't about drafting perfect plans. It was about making change happen by design, not by accident. In his mind, the old playbook was dead: no more endless talking, no more committees—just small, smart actions happening everywhere.

That's the future Bailey had started pitching to clients—because once he saw it, he couldn't unsee it: agentic workflows could turn his big ambitions into tangible actions that scaled naturally. What he failed to see, was that he was selling a future Vic Titious couldn't deliver—a gamble he didn't even recognize.

The Calm Before the Storm

Bailey couldn't contain his excitement. At the next management meeting, halfway through the agenda, he called for a special announcement.

"We've been looking for a breakthrough," he said, his voice steady, energized.

"Well, I've found it."

Around the table, a few heads lifted. Drew leaned back slightly in her chair, curious.

Ira tapped her pen against her notepad.

Bailey launched into his pitch—animated, confident. He spoke about agentic workflows and how they could transform Vic Titious from the inside out.

No more stalled initiatives. No more months of planning with no action. Small teams could lead changes locally—building their own agents using GenAI and easy-to-use no-code platforms—building momentum, showing real results, and setting Vic Titious apart as a modern, nimble firm.

"I've talked to a few clients already," Bailey added, smiling. "They love the idea. And if we can show them how we work differently internally, they'll want us to help them do the same."

He wrapped up triumphantly:

"We're launching this initiative in the next few weeks."

"Questions?"

Ira sat perfectly still, her face giving away nothing.

But inside, she could feel her jaw tighten as Bailey's

words piled up—promise after promise, blind to the canyon between vision and reality.

This is it, she thought. These will be my last weeks at Vic Titious. Bailey clearly is clueless about what he is talking about, let alone what it will take to implement this "breakthrough." Did he really think that projects failed because of her department's involvement?

She barely listened as Bailey answered a few questions, further outlining his grand vision—one sweeping promise after another, how he was going to make money available for a new no-code software platform so everyone would have the necessary tools, and on and on, painting a glowing future where every employee would drive innovation.

Ira grew increasingly weary. Bailey was—or should be—aware that the GenAI tools the firm had bought were used by fewer than 40 percent of the people, and only 10 percent of them were using these tools daily. In other words, fewer than 5 percent of the firm had enough experience with GenAI to even fantasize about agentic workflows. Who exactly did he think would champion all these workflows? And who was going to orchestrate this nightmare?

She gritted her teeth. Ira knew exactly what this "initiative" would mean for her and her team. It sounded eerily similar to the garbage that vendor Van had been peddling for months—buzzwords dressed up as strategy. Agentic workflows making sweeping changes across the firm? Automating improvements locally? It was a nightmare scenario. Especially because she knew that Bailey was also one of those in the leadership team who talked a lot about GenAI but rarely used it himself.

What's more, Bailey seemed oblivious to the fact that the firm's data were a mess—scattered across systems, inconsistently entered, and inconsistently updated. Giving teams free rein to create local automations without guardrails would turn chaos into catastrophe.

Worst of all? In all his glowing talk, he hadn't mentioned funding her team. Not for training and support, not for the two-plus years of work it would take her team just to make something like this viable. No funding for oversight nor for the data cleanup.

Ira glanced at Drew.

Drew wasn't asking many questions either—just nodding slowly, thoughtfully. *Maybe she's hoping this blows over,* Ira thought grimly.

Ira kept her mouth shut. She didn't want to be the drama queen and in any shape or form confirm Bailey's belief that her department was in the way of innovation. She was not going to be the one throwing cold water on yet another Big Idea.

The gap between Bailey's grand vision and her daily reality was just too vast to bridge.

There was one decision left to make. While Bailey saw a future full of possibilities, Ira saw only one way forward—and it led straight out the door. She was exhausted and couldn't muster the energy to try once again to turn someone's unrealistic big vision into reality.

A Door Closed, A Conversation Opened

Bailey was still riding high from the management meeting when Ira knocked on his door the next morning.

She stepped inside, her expression unreadable—neither hostile nor friendly, just carefully neutral.

"Got a minute?" she asked.

Bailey looked up from his computer, still energized from yesterday's announcement. "Of course! Perfect timing, actually. I was just thinking we should start mapping out the implementation timeline for—"

"Bailey." Ira's voice was quiet but firm enough to stop him mid-sentence.

She stepped forward and placed a white envelope on his desk, right on top of the quarterly reports he'd been reviewing.

His stomach dropped. The corporate letterhead. The formal weight of it. He didn't need to open it to know what it was.

"Ira, what—" Bailey started, his instinct kicking in immediately. "Look, if this is about resources, we can figure that out. If it's about the timeline, we can adjust. Whatever you need—"

"Bailey." She said his name again, in the same tone as before. Not angry. Not emotional. Just... final.

He stopped talking. Something about her stance—the way she stood with her hands at her sides, the set of her shoulders—told him this wasn't a negotiation. She wasn't angry. She wasn't bargaining. She was done.

Bailey took a breath, closed his office door quietly, and then sat down.

"Will you help me understand?" he asked, his voice dropping to match hers.

Ira remained standing for a moment, then pulled out the chair across from his desk. "I need you to know this isn't personal," she began. "And it's not about the vision. What did you describe yesterday? It could work. It really could."

"Then why—"

"Because there's a canyon between what you pitched and what it would actually take to make it happen." She looked directly at him. "And I don't think you see it yet."

Ira hesitated. She hated being the downer. Hated being the one to pour water on someone else's excitement, but she was just so exhausted that she no longer cared. While pondering her options the night before, she had decided that if Bailey asked and he seemed genuinely interested—she would give him an honest answer.

Now that the moment was there, she wondered, could she make him see the gulf between his pitch and reality—or would this be another conversation that went nowhere? Ira looked at Bailey, weighing her options. Bailey thrived on bold ideas; Ira weighed risks. Two different instincts—now colliding. Ira didn't have much time to ponder, she had to decide, would it be safe for her to speak up? Since her career was on the line, she decided it was worth a try.

To give herself a few more seconds, she took her time

sitting down across from him. She tried to formulate her thoughts, but then started speaking from the heart.

"I get it," she said. "The vision you pitched—it sounds amazing. Seriously. And I don't want to be the one standing in the way."

She paused, getting her thoughts organized. "But... there's a reason why things are the way they are."

Bailey listened, arms folded—guarded, but still open. "What is the biggest blocker?" he asked.

"Priorities," Ira said. "My team—we're already spread thin. The sustainability initiative to implement policies for data retention, deletion, and storage to reduce unnecessary data accumulation and associated energy costs, we haven't even touched it yet. It'll go straight back to the end of the list if we add this. What's more, the GenAI adoption has not even been completed—everyone has the tools, but only 40 percent are actually using them. So, it doesn't seem realistic to talk about winning Olympic gold while some of our employees are still afraid of the water and all others are still learning to swim."

Bailey nodded, encouraging Ira to go on.

"We also lack capacity and capability. You're talking about setting up local automations. That means our staff and our employees need training—not just how to use tools, but how to think about data, privacy, compliance, project management, maintenance, etc. Right now, we don't have that. Not even close."

Bailey leaned forward. "Alright, what else?"

"Security. Every integration, every bot, every local

process—it opens the door for hackers. Without rigorous checks, one bad setup could expose client data or violate contracts. These risks aren't theoretical."

Bailey sensed that Ira wasn't done, yet. He encouraged her to continue.

And Ira did. "You didn't mention funding once. You mentioned the cost of the no-code platform itself that you propose we use for these agentic workflows. But honestly, that platform may be the cheapest part, as some of what you envision could perhaps be accomplished within our current Microsoft suite. What will drain the time and energy of my team is everything around it—things like integration, security vetting, and training. And then we are not even talking about the cost of getting fee-earners from the various business departments involved. Realistically? You're looking at five times the sticker price, minimum."

Since Ira was on a roll, she decided to also vent her final and perhaps biggest concern. "And last… I am most worried about the execution.

Who's going to run this initiative?

Coordinate between departments?

Prioritize deployments?

Train users?

Maintain these workflows over time?"

After she had spilled everything out on the table that had kept her up at night, Ira felt relieved. Some of the heavy weight she had been carrying around lifted. She also knew there was unlikely to be a way back, and she shook her head gently. "It's not that it can't be done, Bailey. It can. But not by wishing it into existence."

Bailey sat back in silence and deep thought.

He realized—painfully—that he had only seen the upside: the opportunity to position Vic Titious as a leader. He hadn't grasped the full scope or efforts the implementation would take. He'd always respected Ira—she had rarely been wrong. At the same time, her complaints made him wonder if she was the right leader to spearhead this transformation. Should he try to keep her? It seemed she was approaching GenAI as just another tool to adopt. Was she the right person to help Vic Titious navigate this once-in-a-lifetime strategic opportunity?

What other options did he have? Could he hire someone else? Bailey wasn't sure that was going to help—as a new IT director probably would have the same take on things as Ira. No—hiring someone new would just bring even more uncertainty.

So, what was the path forward? Bailey knew how much strain his team was already under and that there were frustrations about past initiatives, but he hadn't realized how little slack they had to absorb any new work and how deeply the frustrations had piled up.

"I'm not trying to kill your idea," Ira said, even softer now. "But if we don't do this right, it'll be just another initiative that fizzles out—and worse, it'll again hurt our best people, those who are trying to make things happen. I don't want to go down that road again."

Bailey was quiet for another long moment—he sensed Ira was giving him negotiation room. That her letter was perhaps not as final as it seemed an hour ago. He reevaluated his options. The concerns she had were all valid points that he needed to do something with, regardless. So it was probably best to find a way to keep Ira on board, instead of having to start from scratch.

Finally, he said:

"You're right."

He looked at the envelope on his desk, then back at Ira.

"What can I do to change your mind? Is there perhaps a middle road? The concerns you raised are valid."

Ira wasn't sure what Bailey meant, but allowed herself a small smile. It hadn't happened often that Bailey admitted she was right. And while she had been convincing herself that quitting Vic Titious was the right action to take, she had not slept well last night after making the decision to leave. She had too much history with the firm, invested so much over the past years, that it felt too early to give up. With the weight of all these concerns lifted from her shoulders, the exasperation she had felt before had disappeared too. So she replied, "For what it's worth, I hope there is."

They agreed to take time to talk through what was needed and work together—not to scrap the vision, but to ground it. To move forward, not with blind enthusiasm, but with clear eyes and a solid plan.

Real change, they both realized, wasn't about

dreaming bigger.

It was about building smarter.

Walking Before Running

Ira wasn't sure how serious Bailey was about GenAI until he had freed up a half day to work things through with her. It turned into a long meeting, but when Ira left Bailey's office, she felt… different.

Not exactly happy.

Not exactly relieved.

But different.

They had a real conversation. Bailey pulled up a new management tool he had come across—RISE—and together they used that to discuss priorities and talked real numbers.

Bailey agreed to back her team with more resources—to keep the trains running while she focused on shaping this new initiative and the future of the firm. That alone was exciting.

The GenAI Value Threshold

One of the areas where Ira and Bailey found common ground, was about how to unlock the value from GenAI. Both agreed it wasn't just about strategy or technical capability.

Bailey had been focused on implementation and outcomes. His main question was: How can we turn

GenAI into client value? But Ira made a crucial point—before workflows can deliver results, people need to trust the tools. And trust only comes with hands-on experience.

Ira had seen it firsthand: Drew, who only occasionally used Copilot, struggled to interpret the outputs. She expected Copilot to deliver her the outcome she was looking for and would remain disappointed until the answer was exactly right. Without a shift in mindset—from deterministic to probabilistic thinking—she was unlikely to accept that there could be multiple outcomes and use the tool to identify the best one. Perhaps that explained why GenAI came more easily to someone like Taylor. She had fewer fixed ideas about what the outcome should look like, and she was more willing to compare variations and improve what GenAI produced. Bailey began to see that pushing for outcomes without sufficient usage was premature. Ira, in turn, recognized that proficiency alone wouldn't generate ROI without clear paths to implementation. Together, they saw the full picture: for GenAI to deliver on its promise, the firm needed to build confidence in its use and build structures to turn insights into results.

Ira sketched it out for both of them:

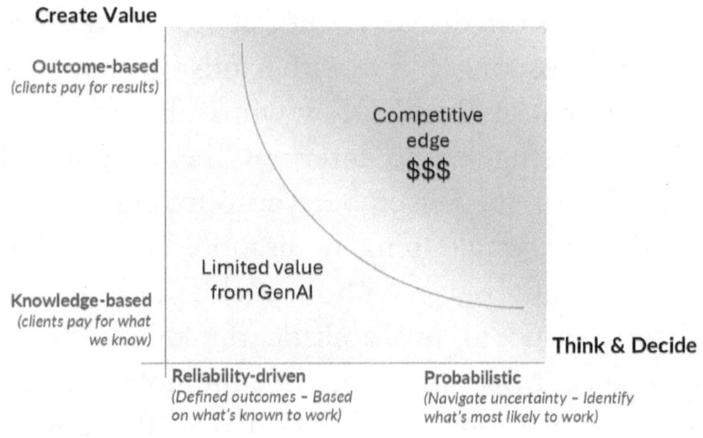

Figure 2: GenAI Value Threshold

The horizontal axis reflected Vic Titious' orientation toward AI: from a deterministic mindset—expecting fixed, reliable outcomes based on what is known to work—to a probabilistic mindset—understanding that GenAI produces variable outputs shaped by context and input. In other words, everyone needed to understand that GenAI gives Vic Titious the opportunity to identify the best variant and solution that is most likely to work, but does not provide a definitive answer.

The vertical axis reflected how Vic Titious creates value. In its current business model clients paid for the knowledge of its experts and they used hourly billing to capture this value. The future—the upper right corner of the graph—reflected the firm's ability to implement solutions that guaranteed outcomes instead of clients paying Vic Titious for what it knew.

Ira marked the curve in the diagram, the "GenAI Value Threshold." Below the curve, the area they currently operated in, they could see that the value from GenAI would be limited or superficial at best. Moving above this curve was where lay sustainable ROI and competitive advantage.

The next question was how to unlock that value. Bailey and Ira agreed to focus on usage of GenAI first and start small with the agentic workflows.

That gave Ira the courage to address Bailey's own familiarity with GenAI—because to her, that seemed like another big problem. How could he make decisions about the future of the firm without having a solid grasp of what the technology could and couldn't do himself?

"Bailey, I need to ask you something, and I hope you won't take this the wrong way," Ira said, shifting slightly in her chair. "How much hands-on experience do you actually have with these GenAI tools?"

Bailey's jaw tightened almost imperceptibly. "I've tried ChatGPT a few times. Used Copilot for some emails."

"And?"

"Mixed results. Sometimes it's helpful, sometimes it gives me garbage I have to completely rewrite." He shrugged. "Look, I get the concept. I understand the potential."

Ira leaned forward. "But Bailey, you're asking me to bet my team's next two years on technology you've only dabbled with. How can we make strategic decisions about something you haven't really experienced?"

There was a pause. Bailey stared at Ira. Only half joking, he said,

"So what are you suggesting? Should I take a corporate training course? Read through PowerPoints about prompt engineering?"

And of course, Bailey wouldn't be Bailey if he didn't toss the challenge right back at her.

"Look," he said, leaning back in his chair with that familiar edge in his voice, "I want to get better at prompting—but I don't have time to sit through some training full of tips and best practices I'll have forgotten by the next day."

He raised an eyebrow, the competitive spark returning to his eyes. "Give me something that saves me time right away—that helps me actually use GenAI, not just learn about it—and I'm in."

Ira felt a small smile tugging at the corner of her mouth. There was the Bailey she knew how to work with. "Alright," she said. "Challenge accepted."

Using Taylor as the Proxy

With so many unknowns and risks, they needed proof before making any major investments or big promises. The first step would be an internal project—probably with Drew's team. Something contained. Something manageable.

And as much as Ira could see the potential, she also knew her team couldn't—and shouldn't—shoulder it alone.

With the high-level plan becoming clear, the next thing Bailey and Ira discussed was who would do the work. Ira made it clear that the accounting project had lacked a dedicated champion—everyone knew what needed to happen and was hoping someone else would invest the time and effort to do the work. So, making actual hands available became part of the deal.

They ran past a few of the usual suspects, but most simply were already overcommitted or had no experience with GenAI. What's more, both Bailey and Ira felt it was important to get people from the next generation involved.

Taylor was good—sharp, methodical, ambitious. Most importantly, of everyone in the firm, she had the most experience with applying various GenAI tools in her work.

However, Taylor was very junior—she had only been with the firm for a few years. Therefore, the plan was to let Taylor own the day-to-day coordination, with Ira and Drew guiding quietly from behind.

Now, Ira thought, it's time to talk to Drew.

Selling the Problem—Not the Solution

One thing Ira knew—and Bailey was learning—was that you don't sell a solution like agentic workflows to someone like Drew.

You don't walk into her office and say, "Hey, we've got this great new thing for you!"

Because that's not how people buy into change. Especially smart, busy people who already have more on their plates than they can handle. They will see the presented solution as a nice-to-have option and will start doubting anything that is less than perfect. Since GenAI would never be perfect, starting on this end would get her nowhere.

So, Ira had asked Bailey to help her work through the outcomes. What problems that Drew was facing could be solved with GenAI and agentic workflows? Together they made a list:

- An overworked team
- Rising pressure to deliver more with less
- Client expectations changing faster than internal capabilities could keep up with

The next step was to tie the project objectives to her pain points—and Drew's goals.

If the project would make Drew's team 10 percent more productive without hiring more staff, Vic Titious would be able to create better margins, serve clients better, and protect its competitive edge.

If Drew agreed, only then would Ira suggest tools and how to make it happen. Ira knew that was the best way to create buy-in, to make change stick—but now she had to apply it in practice.

Ira straightened her shoulders and headed down the

hall toward Drew's office.

This conversation might not be easy, she thought.

But it's the only way to move forward—and this time, we're doing it right.

Ira knocked once and stepped into Drew's office.

"Got a minute?"

Drew looked up from her laptop, wary but curious.

"Sure. Is this about Bailey's grandiose plans?"

Ira gave a small smile. Word traveled fast around Vic Titious. She and Drew had already spoken briefly after the management meeting—enough for Drew to know something was coming. She may have even sensed that Ira had been ready to quit. Her long meeting with Bailey had not gone unnoticed either.

Ira didn't waste time. "I know you're stretched thin. Your team's overloaded, and the pressure's not letting up."

Drew nodded and shrugged—"Nothing new there."

Ira then paused and added:

"I think if we work together, we can change things for the better. My team could help—without becoming a huge additional burden, and it would be aligned with Bailey's big, bold vision."

Drew's face said it all—she looked at Ira like she'd completely lost it, clearly worried about whatever Kool-Aid she'd been drinking.

"I spoke with Bailey, and honestly, it was the first time I felt he listened. We agreed on kicking off a small internal project first, because of all the unknowns around agentic workflows. The goal would be to free up about 10 percent more capacity so your team can keep delivering at a high level without burning out. A collaboration to find smarter ways to cut the noise and improve workflows."

Drew leaned back slightly, her curiosity getting the better of her.

"How?" she asked—her face still frowned. It was always frustrating when outsiders thought they knew better how to run her department than she did. If an easy button existed, she would have found and pressed it a long time ago. However, she trusted Ira. Ira usually was pretty respectful and realistic about what was possible and what was not.

"That's what I want to figure out with you," Ira said. "GenAI is truly a breakthrough technology. We ought to take advantage of that. As I'm not sure exactly what the solution will look like, I suggest we start small. While I'd want you to champion the project, because you know best what will and won't work, I know you have too much on your plate to get fully involved."

"If it is okay with you, I'd love for Taylor to work with me as your proxy. In parallel, my IT team will be helping to get more people in your department comfortable with using GenAI solutions to speed up their work—and I will work with Taylor to develop and introduce agentic workflows in those areas where it makes most sense."

Without missing a beat, Ira continued, "Bailey is willing to support her hours. You'll stay in control, and

Taylor would be freed up to give input and help with the development work on behalf of your team. And instead of an unlimited commitment, we'll just try it for 90 days. If it works—great. If not, none of us will have risked anything major."

Drew tapped her pen on the desk, thinking.

Ira took advantage of that moment to pitch something she wanted to see happen. "There's one catch, though," she said. "Bailey's willing to invest resources to explore how GenAI can help your team tackle its current challenges—but only if you get hands-on experience with GenAI yourself too. Do not just take a course. He wants you to actually *use* it, so when it's time to make decisions, you'll have a real sense of what's possible—and what's not."

The last point wasn't something Bailey had actually said—but truly, both needed to start using GenAI in their daily work if this project was ever going to be successful, Ira thought.

Drew had been able to see the vision Bailey had pitched, but not the execution. His description had sounded too much like another shiny idea that would dump work on her team. So she had kind of thought and hoped it would all blow over like all the other big initiatives.

But this?

This sounded desirable. Grounded.

Manageable.

And with the right people involved—she could see it

happen. She did want to protect Taylor, though.

Finally, she said:

"Okay. Let's talk. I like the setup. But if we want to make it worth Taylor's while, it should be a career-advancing learning opportunity. Could we, for example, make her the project lead—so she has something to add to her CV and can hone her leadership skills, regardless of what comes out of the project?"

Ira let out a breath she hadn't realized she was holding. Drew wasn't talking about if. She was talking about how.

But they both knew something else: If this project was going to work, the team structure had to be designed deliberately. Not perfectly—just realistically.

Why GenAI Adoption Teams Struggle in Firms Like Vic Titious

Innovation theory celebrates heavyweight teams—stable, cross-functional groups with authority, time, and senior backing. A firm like Vic Titious struggles to form such teams: client work cannot be paused, the work is too customized for centralized solutions, and anything built outside a practice group risks being dismissed. As a result, lightweight teams—part-time contributors coordinating across functions—are the norm. The question is, how to make such teams work.

Three insights matter most:

1. **Sponsorship Creates Credibility**

Lightweight teams need a visible ambassador, to secure access, signal priorities, and shield the work when client demands compete with it. In Drew's pilot, Taylor drives the work and Ira coordinates, but only Drew's sponsorship gives the effort institutional weight.

2. **Legitimacy Determines Whether People Engage**

Teams gain traction when projects are clearly tied to client value or firm performance. Links to Drew's department's workload and profitability will give the project legitimacy inside the firm.

3. **Short Sprints Turn Team Changes into Strengths**

Because availability shifts with the client work load, stable membership is unrealistic. Short, structured sprints (30–90 days) allow roles to shift without derailing progress. It brings fresh perspective while preventing burnout.

Creating the team

Drew leaned back in her chair, absorbing the implications.

"We're not building a task force," she said slowly. "We're building a project team that fits our reality."

"Exactly," Ira replied. "We don't want a task force that will just meet and discuss. And I am well aware that no one can afford to step fully out of client work for this project. But if the roles are clear and the support is visible, a project team like this could actually deliver results."

Drew considered this, then nodded. "Let's work with the people who are interested in GenAI and who we can make available. I'll be the sponsor. You coordinate. And Taylor"—she tapped her pen on the table—"Taylor should be asked to lead the day-to-day."

Ira smiled. "She'll need your visible backing."

"I will make sure she has it," Drew said. "If she's going to take on this responsibility, it should be meaningful for her. A genuine leadership opportunity, not just extra work. In addition, since she has never led an initiative like this before, perhaps we should also offer her to participate in a project management course?"

The decision settled between them. The team wasn't perfect. It wasn't fully resourced. But it was aligned with how Vic Titious functioned, not how a textbook imagined innovation to be.

And now that the team structure was set, the next step wasn't to build something.

It was to figure out what needed to be true for the project to be worth scaling.

That meant beginning not with tasks, but with assumptions. Not with a detailed plan, but with a disciplined way to test whether agentic workflows could realistically make Drew's team at least 10 percent more productive—without adding headcount and without compromising security or stability.

Discovery-Driven Planning

The next morning, Ira called Drew and Taylor into a small conference room. A whiteboard, three markers, and a full pot of coffee waited on the table.

"Before we build anything," Ira began, "we need to get clear on what has to be true for this pilot to be worth scaling. That means flipping how we normally plan."

Taylor raised an eyebrow. "Flipping it how?"

"Discovery-Driven Planning," Ira said. "Instead of assuming the solution works, we assume nothing works until it's proven."

She wrote three bullets on the board:

- Start with the desired results and work backward
- Treat every assumption as something to be tested
- Invest bigger only after early evidence shows it's safe

Drew nodded slowly. "Makes sense. So what does that look like for us?"

1: Reverse Income Statement

"First," Ira said, "we define success in hard numbers—before we talk about effort."

Together, the three of them worked through the math.

Target Outcome:

Make Drew's 20-person team 10 percent more productive.

Baseline Assumptions:

- Average internal hourly rate = $150/hour
- Each team member bills on average 1,500 hours/year
- 20 people × 1,500 hours = 30,000 billable hours/year

10 percent Productivity Gain:

- 10 percent of 30,000 hours = 3,000 hours/year saved
- 3,000 hours × $150/hour = $450K of potential value per year

After they had spelled it out this way, Taylor's eyes widened. "That's… a big number, bigger than I expected." "That's why we start here," Ira said. "It tells us the size of the prize."

2: Affordable Loss for the Pilot

"Now we flip to the other side," Ira continued. "What can Vic Titious stand to lose if this pilot project doesn't work? That is, what are we willing to invest and lose to learn if this project has legs?"

Drew didn't hesitate.

"Keep it tight. We're experimenting."

They agreed on a cap of $50K. Small enough to lose without major pain for Drew's department or Vic Titious, while big enough to learn critical lessons about the usefulness of agentic workflows.

3: Scope within the $50K Cap:

Goal: Confirm security viability + build and pilot one working agentic workflow

Budget Breakdown:

Deliverable	Budget Allocation
Increase the adoption of GenAI to build trust & familiarity with these tools	$10K
Security and IT assessment (internal + external checks)	$10K
Taylor's project time (partial backfill, project setup)	$10K
Build and pilot one workflow in a safe, non-critical process	$20K
Total	**$50K**

Taylor wasn't so sure. "There are a lot of assumptions we are making here. Like, that we are able to use a free trial of a low-code/no-code platform, while we don't even know which solution we will be testing or what our requirements are."

"Exactly, you are a step ahead of us, Taylor," Ira said, "listing our assumptions is what we should do next."

4: Assumptions to Test

"Let's list all the assumptions we're making—the things that have to be true for this pilot to succeed."

They filled more than a page together and then rated each assumption for its impact on the project:

Critical

- Team members must use GenAI daily → no experience will result in lack of trust in agentic workflows
- Security of the used tools must be guaranteed → stop the project instantly if not
- Taylor must be able to spend sufficient time on the project → otherwise reprioritize or appoint a new project lead

High

- At least one workflow can be built in 90 days → otherwise no justification to scale the process

Medium

- Drew's department will engage if the new workflow is simple and relevant
- A free trial no-code platform can support the basic build

Taylor looked up. "So every assumption becomes a checkpoint."

"Exactly," Ira said. "This list will keep us focused."

5: High-Level Milestones

Drew uncapped a marker. "Let's put some dates on this." She started drafting a 90-day path:

7 days: Confirm roles, start upskilling Taylor, choose workflow
30 days: Team enrolled in GenAI habit-building; security sign-off; workflow selected
60 days: Workflow built and tested
90 days: Evaluate → scale, pivot, or stop

6: Immediate Next Actions (Next 7–30 Days)

Taylor, sensing that she would have to do the bulk of the work, took over the marker from Drew, and asked, "What would you like me to get started with?" The to-do list quickly grew, but fortunately it was not just all on her:

Next 7 Days:

- Drew will formalize Taylor's role
- Taylor will ask HR about suitable project management courses
- Taylor and Drew will select a candidate workflow (something internal and low risk)

Next 30 Days:

- Taylor will find a GenAI program and enroll Drew's department
- Taylor and Ira will identify one to three no-code platforms
- Ira will perform IT security checks on the selected no-code platform(s)

Taylor glanced at the whiteboard, the project starting to take shape. "Thanks for walking us through this, Ira," she said. "It's focused. Contained. I can see how to actually move forward now."

Drew nodded in agreement. "It's the first plan I've seen in a while that fits our reality: time-bound, disciplined, and small enough to manage."

Ira allowed herself a small smile. "It doesn't guarantee success. But it guarantees we'll learn what we need to know."

The plan wasn't perfect. But it was clear, grounded, and—most importantly—doable.

From Idea to Pilot Project

Bailey sat back after reviewing the updated plan the three had brought him. The reverse income statement. The $50K cap. The clear assumptions to test. The milestone-driven approach, with no vendor lock-in yet.

He took the time to process what he was reading. This wasn't the grand vision he'd pitched to the leadership team. It was something else entirely—but it was real.

"You know what strikes me about this?" he said when reviewing the plan with Ira the next day. "Three weeks ago, I was ready to announce a firm-wide transformation. If you hadn't walked into my office…"

He shook his head slightly. "I would have committed us to a solution I had no business committing to."

Ira waited, letting him work through it. It seemed that Bailey had really listened to her.

"This plan looks good," Bailey continued, tapping the document. "These goals feel like something we can actually deliver on, and they leave enough flexibility to figure out what the solution should look like."

He looked directly at Ira. "I'm willing to put $50K into this. Real money, not just a budget line that gets moved around when other priorities come up."

"And the support structure?" Ira asked. "Because if we're going to do this right—"

"I'm willing to offer support," Bailey interrupted. "Make sure Taylor gets what she needs. Clear obstacles. Make the calls that need to be made."

He paused, a slight smile crossing his face. "And I especially like that you and Drew made it explicit that Taylor agreed to become the project manager. That she was invited—as Drew's proxy—and not voluntold."

While Ira understood what he was hinting at, she wanted Bailey to say it explicitly. So she asked, "Why so?"

"It matters a lot. Half our initiatives fail because we assign people to lead things they don't believe in." Bailey leaned forward. "Taylor said yes to this because she sees the opportunity. That's worth more than any budget allocation."

Preparing to get started

Rather than make a firm-wide announcement, Bailey chose to keep the pilot small for now, sharing it only with leadership and with Drew's team, where the work would actually happen.

A public announcement would have signaled strong support—but it also would have put Taylor in the spotlight far too early.

Better to let the next 90 days unfold quietly, and give her the space she needed to gain momentum.

Why Celebrating Small Wins Matters

When Bailey approved the project, Drew offered to host a small dinner at her home. She had learned from the sustainability initiative that early recognition mattered—it wasn't about declaring victory early, but about signaling that the effort itself mattered.

A small gesture. A show of support. A way to tell Taylor: *You're not doing this alone.*

And in the back of her mind, Drew wondered—if this approach worked, perhaps her sustainability project might find new life too.

One step at a time.

The real work was still ahead.

Why Good Ideas Get Lost (and How to Find Better Ones)

As always, Bailey's presence was bigger than big during the dinner conversation, no change there. To Drew's surprise, however, he started not with a toast to celebrate what they had accomplished so far, but with a dead honest question.

Bailey said, "Alright, I need your help. Before we enjoy the delicious meal Drew has prepared—can someone explain why we're so bad at picking good ideas at Vic Titious? We've started a dozen projects in the past, and most of them evaporated. I want to avoid that happening again at all costs."

Drew leaned against her bookshelf, arms crossed like a shield. Taylor slid into the chair farthest away. Ira hesitated, and then, spoke first.

"It's not just us. There's actual research on this. Humans—and experts especially—are terrible at spotting breakthrough ideas early."

Drew tilted her head, a wry smile tugging at her mouth. "Experts? As in… Bailey?" She shot him a quick grin.

Bailey raised an eyebrow. And responded, "Careful!"

Ira quickly continued, "Both of you, actually. Riedl and colleagues call it the paradox of expertise. The more experienced you are, the harder it is to recognize the value of something that breaks the norms you helped build."

Taylor nodded slowly. She'd seen that expression Bailey wore during idea pitches—the polite, skeptical one that said *convince me.* "That makes sense. Early ideas are always fuzzy. They're not fully formed. Half the time I can barely articulate them myself."

Bailey sighed. "Perhaps, but if it's not crystal clear, it's hard to know what I'm approving."

To which Ira responded, "And that's the second issue: when evaluation is informal, intuition does most of the work. Which means biases sneak in—preferences, past experience, and internal politics."

Drew, still standing, added with a shrug: "And novelty gets filtered out in favor of whatever feels familiar. Remember when accounting wanted to roll out e-billing way back when. We only agreed when we as partners saw it solve an actual problem."

"Exactly. That's why we anchored this pilot to a 10 percent efficiency gain instead of a specific solution. If we judged the idea too early, we'd kill it," Ira said.

Drew shifted, uncrossing her arms, now more engaged. "But don't all organizations have this problem?

Why does it feel so amplified at Vic Titious?"

"Because firms like ours make decisions one idea at a time. Manufacturing companies have portfolios—they manage multiple projects simultaneously and expect some failures, some long shots, some sure bets. Bailey doesn't have that luxury. He has one decision in front of him, with no balancing mechanism," Ira said.

Bailey gave a rueful half-smile. "Feels accurate."

Ira leaned forward. "And we don't have R&D teams waiting for assignments. Everything lands on whoever is available—or whoever didn't step back fast enough."

Drew smirked. "Voluntolds, basically." Taylor raised a hand, "Been there, done that." To which Ira continued, "And because we're working inside billable structures, the people with the best ideas are often the ones with the least time to explore them."

Drew let out a quiet breath—the kind that says *you just described my life*.

Ira straightened, her tone shifting from diagnosis to prescription. "From what I read, there's a better way to handle uncertainty: instead of evaluating an idea, our management team could evaluate early actions. Look at what the team does in the first 4–8 weeks. Do they test assumptions? Talk to users? Gather evidence? Progress and facts are easier to evaluate than the idea itself."

Bailey leaned back, considering. "So I should be judging you all on momentum, not promises."

"Exactly. Like you are doing now. Give Taylor a small early budget. Let her learn quickly. Track milestones—

what assumptions she tested, what she discovered, and what changed because of it."

Drew nodded. "That could work. And it doesn't require heroic time commitments." Taylor gave a quirky smile. "And it would give my brilliant and weird ideas a fighting chance."

Bailey sat with this for a moment. The tension in his shoulders eased. "I like it. It takes the pressure off me. I don't have to guess or predict which ideas will work based on little to no information. Instead, we can identify, select, and support the project teams who actually show they're making progress."

Drew grinned, "and ideally avoid chasing ten good ideas and delivering none."

There was a ripple of laughter—not at the joke, but at the truth behind it.

For the first time, they all felt aligned. Not optimistic exactly, but grounded. Like they'd finally found a way to work with the messiness instead of pretending it didn't exist.

Bailey then toasted, "to a successful start."

Why This Approval Process Is So Different from Traditional Innovation Practice

As Ira drove home from the dinner, she couldn't help reflecting on how unusual the start of this project had been—at least compared to her experience and what she had read about how innovation was managed in industries like manufacturing or consumer goods.

In those sectors, new initiatives were reviewed as part of a portfolio. Teams competed for resources. Projects were compared, scored, ranked, and funded (or killed) as part of a system.

But Vic Titious wasn't that type of organization. Like most professional service firms, it made innovation decisions one idea at a time, driven not by a formal process but by:

- whoever brought the idea forward
- who supported it, and
- how urgent or compelling the moment felt.

It was an inherently opportunistic process—informal, unpredictable, and messy.

And that was exactly why this project mattered: in a firm where ideas didn't win—teams did, the only real way to de-risk innovation was by supporting the people willing to commit early and test their assumptions fast.

Framing the Offer Using RISE

Bailey pondered very different things on his way home. Even with small bets and smart selection, one truth remains: ideas don't de-risk themselves, he realized.

He recalled the RISE framework and wanted to make sure he had framed the opportunity properly and in a way that would be feasible for Taylor to take the lead. The work could not be just dumped on her lap. He mentally walked through each component:

- **Return**: Taylor will lead a visible initiative tied directly to the firm's future—real business impact. Check.
- **Invest**: The firm would invest $50K, including carving out 5 hours of her workweek specifically for the project. Check.
- **Support**: Taylor would have direct access to Ira, Drew, and himself, which hopefully would help to short-circuit the existing bureaucracy. Drew had also suggested giving Taylor access to an online project management course. Excellent idea, he thought. Check.
- **Expectations**: 90 days. Weekly progress reports. One working pilot workflow. A clear evaluation at the end—no vague, never-ending "innovation project." Check.

Clearly, the project would be extra work for Taylor. She already knew that. She had been doing much of it informally anyway.

The difference now? Bailey realized he was providing a structured, time-limited, career-building opportunity.

The question was, could she handle it? Time would tell, and soon, as the pressure was on.

Part 2 Summary

In professional service firms, moving from an exciting idea to a focused project takes discipline—not just enthusiasm.

Bailey's willingness to listen, set a realistic short-term goal, frame the affordable loss ($50K), and provide support, turned a risky initiative into a clearly defined discovery project.

Taylor wasn't voluntold to lead—she was offered a meaningful role, with clear support and expectations.

By slowing down and planning smartly, the project team gave themselves a real chance to build momentum in a sustainable way.

Key Takeaways

- Start with a business need—not the solution. A clear business need is what should drive each innovation project.
- Discovery-driven planning and the affordable loss principle provide structure when outcomes are uncertain.
- Projects must be framed as opportunities—not burdens—for the people involved, which often means making time and providing additional support, such as in this case, project management support for Taylor.
- Small wins matter—celebrating commitment

builds the foundation for resilience later.

Reflection Questions

How does your organization evaluate ideas and projects?

Think of a recent idea or project you were excited about:

- Did you define success first—or did you jump straight to building?

How do new projects typically get started in your organization?

- Are they framed around business objectives or personal enthusiasm?

When asking someone to drive an innovation project:

- Do you clearly explain the return, investment, support, and expectations (RISE)?
- Or will it be considered part of the job and come across as just more work?

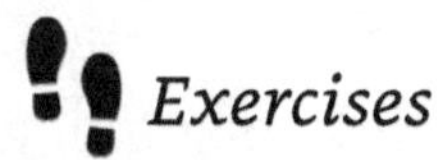

Exercises

Exercise 1: Reverse Your Next Big Idea

Take a GenAI project or initiative you're currently excited about.

- Write down the desired business result first.
- Estimate what that result would be worth.
- Then set your affordable loss: the maximum amount you would invest to test if the idea is viable.

Exercise 2: Craft a RISE Offer

Pick someone you would like to involve in a GenAI project (real or hypothetical).

Write a short offer describing:

- Return (What's in it for them?)
- Invest (What support/resources will they get?)
- Support (Who will help remove obstacles?)
- Expectations (What does success look like—and how much time will it take to get those results?)

Exercise 3: Plan Your Small Win

Think about the first milestone in a current or future project.

- How could you celebrate learning and commitment, not just results?

- Plan a small action (announcement, meeting, acknowledgment) that marks the beginning properly—while setting clear expectations and creating accountability for the next step.

"I'd rather fund something with a realistic return you'll fight to deliver than a number in a business case— an empty promise that gets put in a drawer and never comes out again."

Part 3
Developing the Solution

Excitement Collides with Reality

The project was greenlit. Expectations were high. Taylor had blocked time off in her calendar, ordered an extra pile of sticky notes, and cleaned her whiteboard. She was ready.

All the experimenting on her own time and the tips from Van had given her a pretty good idea of what she wanted to do. Or at least, Taylor thought she did.

The problem was, how and where to start? She opened her laptop and stared at the blinking cursor.

The idea had seemed so clear just yesterday. Now? Not so much.

The outcome was clearly defined—10 percent time savings by optimizing the onboarding process using GenAI. Easier said than done.

From her own experience she knew that onboarding new clients was a frustrating, time-consuming process. It required digging through the firm's internal databases for any relevant client information, searching for additional context online, and cross-referencing all of it with notes from Drew or other partners taken during the intake meeting. Each time, just that part of the process alone took her hours. From there, she needed to identify the client's core challenges, frame them within the broader industry landscape, and craft a tailored proposal for how Vic Titious could help. All together, each proposal took days of Taylor's time—and less than half of them led to actual clients. It was neither efficient nor particularly effective. Worse, Drew was always complaining about how long it took—and clients weren't exactly thrilled with the results either.

Taylor decided to pick up where she left off before the project became "official": with Van.

She hoped Van could help her take the next step. Van had once shown her what was possible—enough to get Taylor started with GenAI.

And, since the use of GenAI had been approved within Vic Titious, she, with the help of Van, had started to experiment a little, pulling client data from the client's website and setting up fake accounts in an accounting system. That's how she'd learned matching was the big bottleneck—and that GenAI could actually handle it.

In the firm's dataset, the same client might be listed as "Vic Titious," "V Titious," or "Vic Titious PLC". Their current system was unaware that these were all names for the same firm, making data collection more complicated than necessary.

This ability to recognize what belonged together and what didn't was what impressed her most about Van's tool. It didn't care about those inconsistencies. It just... worked.

She had been skeptical at first. "What if it confuses Baker and Bakery?" she'd asked.

"It won't," Van had promised. "It's context-aware and as a result 99 percent accurate."

To her surprise, he had been right.

Taylor figured she could just pick up where they left off.

She sent him a quick message:

"Hey! Officially kicking off a pilot project. Can we connect this week to discuss the details?"

The reply came quickly:

"Sure. What's your budget?"

Taylor frowned.

That wasn't the welcome she expected.

"Not sure yet," she replied. "What range are we talking about?"

Van answered:

"Usually the implementation is between $100K and $250K, depending on how much support and training you need from us."

Her stomach dropped. That was two to five times the entire pilot project budget.

Before she could even respond, Van wrote:

"Let me know when you get funding. Happy to chat more then."

Just like that, the conversation was over.

Taylor leaned back in her chair and stared at the ceiling.

What was I thinking? she wondered. *I don't even know how to manage a project.*

Clarity Before Action

Already after a few hours, Taylor considered throwing in the towel. The budget shock, the fruitless search for training, and—most of all—the blinking cursor on the empty page threatened to pull her under. Before the spiral took hold, Drew walked by.

"Got a minute?" Taylor asked, following her to the coffee machine. "What's up?" Drew asked, grabbing a mug.

Taylor hesitated, then everything tumbled out at once.

"I don't know if I can do this. I feel stuck already and I haven't even properly started. I've been digging into GenAI training programs, but honestly? I wouldn't recommend a single one to you or Bailey. And the onboarding solution—I thought I had it figured out, and now it looks like it'll cost five times our budget. I thought I had a plan. Now I just feel… in over my head."

Drew didn't flinch.

"Good," she said.

Taylor blinked. "Good?"

Drew nodded.

"If the solution was easy, we wouldn't be where we are. And if you weren't stuck, you'd probably be rushing in the wrong direction."

She poured her coffee, as if they were discussing nothing more dramatic than a staffing update.

"Here's what I want you to do," Drew continued. "Don't solve anything this week. Don't design. Don't build. Just get clear on what problem you're actually solving."

Taylor raised an eyebrow.

"I mean, talk to people," Drew continued. Five from our team. Two or three from Ira's group. Someone from Finance, if you can swing it. Ask how they currently onboard clients, what slows them down, how do they get or report client data, and what's eating up their time. Don't pitch. Don't defend. Just listen."

Taylor nodded faintly.

"And after you have listened to their stories, write down what you think the problem is," Drew added. "In one sentence. Plain English. If you can't explain it simply, you don't understand it yet."

Taylor nodded slowly. "Okay…I can do that."

"Then ask yourself: if this project is wildly successful, what will have changed? And what's the one metric you'll use to track that? That's your North Star. It will keep you focused."

She paused. "You're not lost, Taylor. You just haven't drawn the map yet and don't have any navigation tools. And this"—she motioned to Taylor's overwhelmed expression—"this is the part where most projects stall. Because people confuse action with clarity."

Taylor gave a reluctant smile. "That's… uncomfortably accurate."

"Take the time to see the full picture," Drew said. "Not just your view as an associate. Pull the right people in and listen."

She hesitated for a beat, then added, "And don't make this a solo effort. Scout more broadly. Post on LinkedIn—ask who knows a program that can help us accelerate GenAI adoption. If you post it, I'll share it with my network too."

Taylor nodded, feeling something she hadn't felt in hours: direction.

Finding the Right GenAI Training Program

Taylor got to work.

When it came to training, she knew exactly what she didn't want. Not another program that opened with a parade of risks and horror stories—she'd seen how quickly that killed enthusiasm. And not the over-polished, "look how magical GenAI is" workshops either. Drew rolled her eyes at those, and frankly, Taylor didn't blame her.

She needed something practical. Something that let people start in the shallow end—safe, everyday tasks where they could experiment without pressure. A program that treated GenAI not as a machine that delivered perfect answers, but as a tool that sparked ideas, generated options, and made work easier a little at a time.

Thanks to Drew's large LinkedIn network, she found one quickly. It focused on turning GenAI into a daily habit—starting small, building trust through usage, not spectacle.

Taylor brought it to Ira.

"I read about the program you found," Ira said, visibly impressed. "That's a great pick."

Taylor smiled. "Took a bit of digging and asking around, but I finally found what I was looking for: low-stakes, practical, something people can ease into."

"Exactly," Ira nodded. "No more polished demos or grand visions. Just daily use. Familiarity. The trust that comes from hands-on experience."

Once Ira approved it, Taylor shared the course with the department. To her surprise, sign-ups started rolling in almost immediately. The promise of "save one hour/ week" certainly didn't hurt.

A few days later, she stopped by Ira's office. "Did you see how many people already signed up? I thought I'd have to chase people down."

Ira chuckled. "A little fear of missing out never hurts. But honestly, I think this gives people permission to explore safely. Low time commitment, low pressure. What I like most is that it teaches people that GenAI isn't supposed to give them the answer—it helps them navigate the unknown."

Taylor tilted her head. "That's been the biggest mindset shift for me. I used to expect perfect answers",

Taylor admitted. “Now I realize it’s more about expanding or narrowing my options. It helps me get unstuck."

"Exactly," Ira said. "We grew up expecting computers to be deterministic—and always right. GenAI is different. It’s probabilistic. It predicts the next word, or the next pixel. It’s surprisingly good if you let it help you think, but infuriating if you expect it to think like you."

Taylor laughed. "That is exactly how it happened for me. And it’s the mindset Drew will need if she’s ever going to trust whatever agentic workflow we build."

Ira nodded, more serious now. "This habit-building takes time. But without it, people won’t trust the outputs of a new workflow—let alone that they can lead these efforts. If they’re already using GenAI daily, already comfortable with its quirks? That would be a game changer."

What People Say vs. What They Actually Do

Doing the interviews was a lot more time-consuming than Taylor anticipated. She also quickly realized they weren’t going to be simple.

Her first question had been innocent enough: "So—can you walk me through the onboarding process?"

Every person smiled politely and gave the same polished answer.

The official steps. The neat sequence. The version written in the Department Handbook Taylor had received when she joined the firm.

Taylor nodded, but inside she thought, there's no way you actually do it like that. I certainly never did.

After the third identical response, she adjusted her approach.

"Okay," she said to the next person, "forget the official process. Tell me about the last client you onboarded. What actually happened?"

That's when everything changed.

The analyst in front of her sighed in relief.

"Oh. Well, that's… different."

She leaned in. "Different how?"

The analyst closed the door.

"Well, the first thing I do is skip Step 3. It's pointless. Nobody has time for it."

Taylor blinked. "Nobody?"

"Not unless you want the partner to yell at you for taking too long."

Another meeting. Another story.

Assistant: "I always start in the CRM—the client system." Taylor: "Why not the pricing database?" Assistant (laughing): "Because it hates me. Half the time it crashes. I only go there if the partner insists."

"Do you have access?" Taylor asked.

The assistant hesitated, then lowered her voice.

"Technically? No. But…" She tapped her notebook. "I have Sam's password."

Taylor stared. "You… share passwords?"

A blush. A shrug. "…It's the only way to get anything done."

And those were not the only revelations.

One partner's assistant reenacted how she patched together four disconnected systems with the same weary gesture every time she mentioned another login screen.

Someone from Ira's group physically recoiled when Taylor mentioned the old pricing system.

"Oh no. Not that beast," he said, shaking his head. "That thing is a security nightmare."

"Then why does everyone still use it?"

"Because it's the only place with the full history. IT thinks nobody touches it anymore." "So, nobody told you in IT?"

He gave her a look. "Would you?"

By the end of the week, Taylor's neat assumption—10 percent time savings—looked ridiculous.

Every assistant burned hours per client stitching data together. Every forecast required detective work. And more than once, someone admitted a missed step had led to… "well, let's just say… expensive surprises."

She wrote in her notebook, underlined twice:

Not just productivity. Compliance risk.

And there was still the elephant in the room: Van's tool could fix most of this—but the price tag still made her stomach clench.

She spent the weekend Googling alternatives. Everything was either missing key features, had terrible reviews, or was priced as high as Van's.

Two weeks later, she walked into Drew's office carrying a stack of notes that felt heavier than paper.

"I did the interviews," she said. "And I may have underestimated the problem. By a lot."

From Faster Reporting to Smarter Action

Drew raised an eyebrow. "Go on."

Taylor walked her through what she'd found—the inconsistent naming, the four unlinked databases, the scraps of notes, the improvised searches. With each example, Drew's expression tightened just a little, as if Taylor were confirming things she'd known but preferred not to say aloud.

"And about 30 percent of our forecasts have been… off," Taylor finished quietly. "Not because of judgment. Just because the data are impossible to piece together."

Drew exhaled slowly. "30 percent…" She rubbed her forehead. "We've tried to fix this before, you know."

Taylor looked up.

"Three times, actually," Drew said. "Once with IT. Once with a data vendor. Once with an internal task force." She gave a dry laugh. "All three failed in different ways."

"What happened?" Taylor asked.

"The same thing that always happens," Drew said. "We tried to standardize something that isn't standard. Everyone wanted a different report. A different view. A different definition of 'client.' And the data was too messy to automate. Every attempt got stuck in endless requirements sessions or blew up in integration."

She paused.

"And honestly, we all just… learned to live with it."

There was no anger in her voice—only the weary acceptance of someone who had been carrying a burden for years.

Taylor hesitated, then said, "I think that's why GenAI could change the equation."

Drew lifted her gaze. "How?"

"It doesn't need perfect data," Taylor said. "It works with what's there. It reasons through inconsistencies instead of forcing us to clean them first. It can match, validate, and surface the right pieces before humans even touch it."

Drew didn't answer right away. She looked almost wary of feeling hope too soon.

"We've heard such promises before," she said softly.

Taylor nodded. "I know. But this is different. I've tested it. Van's software handles mismatched client names effortlessly. With a human in the loop and checking early, we can trust the output without needing a perfectly standardized process."

Drew considered that for a moment.

"So… not a rigid system," she said. "More like… clearing the runway before takeoff. Give people clean data, let them make the judgment calls."

"Exactly."

Drew's posture shifted—not enthusiastic, but no longer defensive. Curious. Cautious. Testing the idea against her experience.

"And previous attempts failed because we tried to automate the entire process," Taylor added. "Agentic workflows don't do that. They automate the messy groundwork so the human work becomes faster, better, more confident."

Drew tapped her pen on the desk.

"So the system doesn't replace judgment. It gets rid of the noise."

"Yes."

Drew leaned back. "That would be… different."

Not a yes.

And not a no.

A small crack in the door—enough for possibility to slip through.

"Cost-wise," Drew said finally, "what are we talking about?"

Taylor grimaced. "That's the part we still have a problem with." As she said it, she noticed something had shifted. She no longer felt lost and drowning; it felt more like she'd stepped onto a bigger stage—and was slowly getting used to how bright the lights were.

Standardized vs. Agentic Workflows

Traditional automation assumes work can be fully defined upfront. But in professional services, every client and case brings unique context. That's why past automation efforts often failed: they required a level of standardization that never existed.

GenAI changes the starting point: It can interpret messy inputs, fill gaps, and adapt to variation—allowing workflows that guide decisions rather than prescribe exact steps.

Topic	Standardized Workflow	Agentic Workflow
Best for	Routine, predictable work	Complex, variable work
Assumes	One best practice upfront	Context shapes decisions
How it works	Follow fixed rules	Adapt with GenAI + human oversight
Success depends on	Compliance	Engagement & judgment
Weakness	Breaks with exceptions	Needs humans mentally involved

That means: GenAI makes it possible to automate messy groundwork without forcing standardization—something earlier systems couldn't do.

Striking Gold (and Knowing What to Do with It)

Drew was quietly impressed.

Taylor had taken the interviews seriously. She'd stayed composed after the Van setback. And most importantly, she hadn't sugar-coated anything.

She still had a lot to learn—especially about not folding at the first sign of resistance—but Drew reminded herself: *She's young. She's learning. And she's doing the real work.*

What surprised Drew most wasn't the problems Taylor uncovered. Drew had known about most of them for years. What surprised her was that Taylor didn't seem to understand the weight of what she'd found.

The issues were bigger than the two of them imagined. But so was the opportunity.

Still, Drew didn't let her face show too much. She'd been here before. More than once.

Every few years, someone tried to "fix onboarding." IT had tried. Operations had tried. Once, even a highly paid boutique consultant had tried. They all came in with confidence, then disappeared quietly when the reality of the data hit them. Nothing was clean. Nothing matched. Everything needed "just a little cleanup" that ballooned into a colossal swamp of exceptions, legacy rules, and undocumented workarounds.

The result was always the same:

A polished slide deck.

A few hopeful meetings.

Then silence.

So yes—she had learned to be cautious with what glistened like gold. Sometimes it glittered right up until you got close and then it turned out to be fool's gold, just pyrite.

But as Taylor talked, Drew couldn't ignore a flicker in her chest. Something she hadn't felt in years. Not optimism—she wasn't foolish enough for that. More like… the possibility of being wrong in the best possible way.

Because buried inside those four chaotic systems was something no competitor had: fifteen years of pricing patterns, client decisions, risk behaviors, margins, and outcomes. It was a treasure trove disguised as clutter. And all these years, their forecasts had never improved as a result of that history, because every new engagement started from scratch—data pulled manually, templates reused, but nothing learned.

If GenAI could reason through messy inputs… If it could match, validate, and surface what mattered…

If an agentic workflow could improve with each forecast…

Then, for the first time, the mess wouldn't be a liability. It would be an advantage.

Not clean data.

Context-rich data.

She tried to imagine what that would mean for clients—more accurate predictions, better decisions, perhaps even fixed-fee engagements with higher margins.

It was the kind of strategic shift leaders talked about at conferences but she had never quite managed to pull off. To turn this data into a real opportunity, though, there were a lot of ifs.

Drew knew better than to let herself run away with the dream.

Not yet.

Not without proof.

Not without hearing from the clients who had lived the consequences of their shaky forecasts.

She didn't want to give Taylor false hope—or worse, embarrass them both.

"If we can link these databases with 90 percent accuracy," Taylor said, "that alone would save everyone hours. And if Van's claim of 99.8 percent holds, maybe the price tag isn't as impossible as I thought." She paused. "This could be huge. Not just for our team—for everyone."

Then her confidence wilted a little. "Unless the pricing is still totally out of reach. I mean, the $200K doesn't even include integration or support."

Drew nodded, grounding them both.

"Exactly. Which is why we need a broader plan before we take this anywhere. Ira will never approve a software spend like that without knowing the full scope. And honestly?" She took a breath. "Neither will I."

The gold shimmered.

But Drew knew better than to grab it with both hands.

This time, they needed some form of evidence.

And a process.

And a plan that could survive contact with reality.

Understanding the Full Cost of a Solution

Drew picked up her coffee and leaned back. "I do not want another accounting or sustainability debacle," she said. "We underestimated everything—the time, the cleanup, the hand-holding. Twice. I'm not doing that again."

Taylor looked up, surprised. Drew didn't usually open the vault this wide.

"We kept saying the vendor was expensive," Drew continued. "Turns out the vendor was the cheapest part."

Taylor frowned. "What do you mean?"

Drew gave a rueful laugh. "Ira might know other tools, or whether we could build something ourselves. But no matter what we choose, we need her help to figure out the real cost."

Taylor tilted her head. "The licensing fee?"

"No," Drew said. "The actual cost."

Taylor waited.

"Integration," Drew said, ticking off fingers. "Training. Getting IT to support it. Getting you to support it."

Taylor snorted. "Wait—I'm not free?"

"Not even remotely," Drew said. "Your time, my time, IT's time, operations' time… all of that gets paid from somewhere. The vendor won't mention any of that on their invoice, so people pretend it doesn't exist."

Taylor grimaced. She hadn't thought about that. At all.

Drew took another sip. "That's what burned us before. We obsessed over the price tag in the proposal, but never once asked, 'Whose nights and weekends will this eat?' Or, 'What tools won't talk to each other?' Or, 'Who's going to be dragged into this at the worst possible moment?'"

Taylor winced. "So… talk to Ira about what will actually be involved?"

"Exactly," Drew said. "And anyone else who's going to get pulled in—willingly or not. If we surface the real costs now, we can make smart decisions. And maybe—maybe—for once, we won't blow the timeline or the budget."

Taylor nodded slowly. "Makes sense. It's not just what we buy—it's what it takes to make it actually work."

Drew raised her mug in a half salute. "Welcome to the part of the job that never gets advertised."

She set the mug down and leaned back, staring at the ceiling for a moment before focusing on Taylor again.

"So we're not done," she said quietly. "Not even close."

Validating the Case for Change

"There's a lot more for us to sort out," Drew

continued, straightening in her chair. The fatigue was still on her face, but her mind was clearly running at full speed. "Before we go anywhere near asking for budget, we need two things: external validation and feasibility."

Taylor nodded cautiously. Drew rarely spoke in such direct terms.

"Start with competitors," Drew said. "If firms like ours are already offering faster intake or better forecasting, we need to know. And if they aren't… well, that tells us something too."

Taylor jotted a note, but Drew wasn't done.

"I'll talk to a few clients," she said, almost to herself.

Taylor looked up. "Our clients?"

"Yes," Drew said. "Because if we're asking the firm to spend this much money, we have to prove the value goes beyond our own headaches. Faster intake sounds great to us. But would clients value it? Would they pay more for it? Would it change their experience?"

She paused, debating how honest to be.

"And forecasting…" Drew sighed. "If our clients had better visibility earlier, what would that unlock? Faster go/no-go decisions? More accurate budgeting? Less back-and-forth? If this workflow doesn't move the needle for them, we shouldn't build it."

Taylor frowned. "I thought this was about internal efficiency."

"It is," Drew said. "But internal efficiency alone doesn't get funding. Efficiency that clients feel—that's what changes the game. If clients move faster, we move faster. If they trust our predictions, they rely on us more. That's the multiplier."

Taylor nodded slowly. She'd never thought of it that way.

"And before we start cheering for Van's solution," Drew continued, "we need to check our assumptions. We might be solving the wrong problem. Or we might be ignoring a bigger one. Clients will tell us—if we're willing to hear the truth."

She tapped her pen lightly on the desk.

"Same with vendors," she added. "Not to shop. To understand what's actually feasible. What exists. What's overpriced. What's vaporware. It keeps us from building castles on clouds."

Taylor scribbled faster.

"And internal users?" she asked.

"Oh, we go back to them too," Drew said. "But with sharper questions. Now that you've seen the real mess, we can ask what's essential, what would genuinely change their day, and what would be wishful thinking."

Taylor let out a slow breath. On the one hand, this felt overwhelming. On the other, it felt… grounded. Doable. Necessary. Smart.

Back at her desk, she wrote down a list of names:

Vendors she'd come across over the past weeks.

Two clients Drew trusted.

A few colleagues who never sugarcoated anything.

Just then, her project management course pinged on her screen.

Module 1: Setting High-Level Goals—complete.
Module 2: Conducting Stakeholder Interviews—complete.
Module 3: Surfacing Assumptions and Testing Them—in progress.

Taylor smiled.

For once, the timing made perfect sense.

Setting the Example

Taylor didn't know it yet, but she wasn't just building a workflow anymore.

She was building a prototype for how the entire firm might change.

Drew knew it.

Ira definitely knew it.

And Bailey—whether he'd admit it or not—had been waiting years for someone to manage a pilot project that didn't collapse under its own complexity.

That was why the early steps mattered so much.

A pilot project wasn't supposed to solve everything.

It was supposed to answer the questions that kept decision-makers frozen:

Is this worth investing in?

Will anyone actually use it?

Does it move the needle for clients?

What would it take to make it real?

If a pilot couldn't answer those questions, it didn't create momentum; it created noise.

Noise meant hesitation.

Hesitation meant no budget, no progress, no change.

Drew had seen it too many times.

So before looping in vendors or dragging other teams into the effort, she wanted this pilot to do what pilot projects rarely did at Vic Titious: generate clarity, not confusion.

Clear goals.

A measurable outcome.

A way to show—simply and credibly—what changed.

It wasn't about building fast.

It was about learning early and learning quickly. And if they got that right, Taylor's small project could become the pattern for everything that came after.

Vendors Need Proof Too

Van wasn't sure what to make of the email.

Taylor's message was polite, confident, and—he had to admit—far more detailed than the midnight notes she used to send him. She included a summary of the interviews, a clear articulation of the problem, and a request: Could they pilot his system for free using a small internal dataset?

It wasn't the first time she'd asked for a favor. As long as she was experimenting on her own time, he'd happily tossed her pointers. She was a friend. But company resources were different. Those weren't his to give away.

And he'd learned the hard way that *"we're serious"* could mean anything from "we'll sign next week" to "we lost the budget but forgot to tell you."

He had pushed back earlier because, frankly, her outreach felt naïve. She didn't grasp what she was getting into. But this time… something was different.

Drew's name was copied.

So was Ira's.

That made him pause.

Taylor had clearly mapped the workflow. She had identified the bottlenecks. She had described the opportunity in concrete terms. She wasn't playing anymore.

Still, he wasn't ready to jump in.

"Appreciate the note," he wrote back.

"What would be next after this? Is there budget for a $200k investment?"

Her answer came a few hours later—honest, unpolished, and unexpectedly persuasive.

"Honestly, I don't know yet. With what we know today, definitely not. Too many unknowns. But if I can prove the value, I think we stand a real chance. For now, we only need access to test your matching engine. If it works, I can build the case."

Van rubbed his temples.

She was junior—very junior.

Could she influence a six-figure decision?

He doubted it.

But the sample data she'd sent earlier?

If she was even half right about the time wasted, the manual matching, the inconsistencies…

Well, *that* had caught his attention.

Another client had justified the purchase the exact same way.

He typed slowly.

"Okay. What about a one-month paid trial for $5k?

You build the manual sample. We run it through the engine. But if we meet the benchmark, I want Vic Titious to commit to next steps."

Taylor was thrilled.

Then immediately panicked.

Could she make a commitment like that?

Turning a Hypothesis into a Test

Taylor sat staring at the draft pilot plan, feeling utterly out of her depth.

The cursor blinked like it was taunting her.

Ira walked by again and paused. "Still negotiating with the void?"

Taylor exhaled. "Van wants success criteria. Real ones. And I don't know how to define them. I've never run a pilot."

Ira nodded. "Then don't pretend you have. Ask him. Vendors run pilots all the time. Let him help frame the test. You just make sure it works in our world."

Taylor stared at her. "…I can do that?"

"Please," Ira said. "It's expected."

That afternoon, Taylor joined a call with Van—steadier than before, but still unsure.

"So," Van began, "what are your success metrics?"

Taylor swallowed. "Can… you help me with that? I don't want to set unrealistic benchmarks or test the wrong thing. You've done this more than I have."

Van didn't laugh. He softened.

"Of course. Most pilots fall apart because success isn't clearly defined. Let's design this together."

Relief washed over her.

"Okay," she said, "what do you typically measure?"

"For matching?" Van said. "Accuracy. Always accuracy first. If the engine can match entities across systems correctly, everything else—speed, workflow improvements—comes later."

Taylor nodded, grateful for something concrete.

"So how about this," he continued. "You build a small manual sample across your four systems. We'll run our engine on the same sample. Then we compare line by line. If we hit 95 percent accuracy, that's success. If we exceed it, even better. If we miss it—you walk away."

"And speed?" Taylor asked.

"Not yet," Van said. "Worrying about processing time comes later. Let's focus on reliability. Solve the foundation first."

Taylor exhaled. "That feels… real. Measurable."

"And fair," Van added. "For both sides."

He paused, then shifted tones.

"But before I agree to anything formal, I need the people involved who can approve next steps. I can't run a pilot based on junior enthusiasm alone—no offense."

"None taken," Taylor said quickly.

"I'd like Ira and Drew in the room," Van said. "We all need to be aligned. Otherwise we hit the benchmark and still will go nowhere."

Her stomach tightened—but this time, it felt like forward motion.

"I'll set it up."

The Calibration Meeting

A few days later, Taylor sat in a small conference room with Ira and Drew as Van joined by video. The energy was different now—steadier, more serious.

Van walked them through the approach.

"You'll create a representative manual sample across the four systems," he said. "We'll run our engine on the same sample. Then we compare line by line. 95 percent is the threshold."

"And if you exceed it?" Drew asked.

"Then we talk next steps."

"And if you don't?" Ira said.

"Then you walk away. No pressure."

Drew nodded. "Fair."

Only then did Van add, "To run this properly, we'll need a small paid trial. Five thousand for one month, or eight thousand for two."

Drew and Ira exchanged a look Taylor couldn't decode, but she sensed it mattered.

Drew turned to her. "Two months gives us room to breathe."

Ira nodded. "And to repeat the test if we need to."

"Alright," Drew said. "Two months."

Van smiled. "Then let's do it."

After a few more details got sorted out, Vic Titious committed to an $8K pilot.

It wasn't cheap. It limited their ability to try other tools this year.

But it bought them something far more valuable:

Options, insights, and a quick way to learn more.

Taylor didn't yet understand why that mattered so much.

But she was about to.

Taylor Builds the Test

For the next few weeks, Taylor lived in spreadsheets.

She pulled a small, representative sample from each database—CRM, accounting, the web archive, and the ancient pricing system—and created a master list by hand.

It was painful work.

The naming inconsistencies were worse than she'd imagined. At one point, she spent almost two hours untangling what turned out to be two different clients with near-identical names.

When she finally ran the data through Van's engine,

she held her breath.

The results came back slowly—ten times slower than Van had projected.

But the accuracy?

99.8 percent.

Taylor triple-checked. It held.

The engine even caught a duplicate she had missed.

She flagged it for Ira.

Ira Sees the Risk Behind the Win

"This is promising," Ira said when Taylor showed her the results.

"But the processing lag worries me. If this is slow on a small test set, what happens when we scale?"

Taylor nodded. "Speed will have to come next. But the accuracy's real. This means we could create forecasts that make sense—and that people might actually trust."

Ira tilted her head. "Have you shared this with Drew yet? I'm curious what she will say."

Drew's Growing Understanding of GenAI

Drew wasn't so sure.

"99.8 percent accuracy… what does that mean in practice?" she murmured.

Her GenAI training had changed how she interpreted numbers like that. She'd started cautiously: email rewrites, meeting summaries. But lately she'd pushed further—

co-writing documents, reframing arguments, exploring options.

Some outputs had been astonishingly helpful. Others had been confidently wrong—fabricated sources, made-up facts, answers that sounded right but weren't.

It was a reminder she couldn't ignore:

GenAI wasn't a truth engine.

It was a prediction engine.

Still, she couldn't deny how much it helped her think faster, explore more angles, get unstuck. And if the matching engine really delivered 99.8 percent accuracy...

This workflow might let them reconfigure how they priced onboarding. Maybe even move toward fixed fees without risking their margins.

The idea was intoxicating—and terrifying.

The workflow still had friction. It required teams to provide inputs earlier, make decisions earlier, think earlier. If that slowed people down instead of speeding them up, would anyone use it?

The promise was big.

But did it have pull?

Doubt, Responsibility, and the Next Step

As Drew wrestled with the implications, Taylor asked, "Drew—what did you learn from our clients?"

Drew grimaced. "Good point. I haven't had a chance yet."

It was true. A personnel issue had swallowed her

whole. She hated that her delay meant they were moving with half the picture.

"You did well," Drew said, in an attempt to distract Taylor. "Now let's be smart. We need Bailey in the loop, but not before we understand the full cost. I want Ira's input first."

She then hesitated. "And I will reach out to those clients. Their perspective will help us understand whether this plan has real value—or just internal appeal."

Taylor nodded.

They were both cautiously excited. There was still a long road ahead. But for the first time, it felt real: They were building the firm's first agentic workflow—one that could reshape how new client work began, deliver better outcomes, and save everyone hours.

The Commitment Conversation

Taylor poured everything she had into the business plan to justify the $200K investment in Van's solution.

Armed with GenAI, she crafted a crisp proposal—complete with high-level goals, investment breakdowns, assumptions, milestones, and a projected five-year ROI.

The numbers were bold.

$100K for performance testing. $200K for Van's solution, and another $150K for full integration.

In total, a $450K investment that would not only boost productivity by 10 percent, but also enable accurate forecasting—unlocking a level of predictability that, until now, had been an elusive dream. That same predictability could even make fixed-fee services feasible.

The investment would be earned back in about two years, which should make it worthwhile. To further substantiate that it was worth it, Taylor had extrapolated the revenue predictions for the next five years, and that showed a 10x ROI—aligned with what her project management course said it should be.

When she rehearsed the pitch, Drew and Ira offered polite nods, a few suggestions on wording—but no critique of the numbers, which unnerved her more than if they had pushed back.

Were the numbers too aggressive?

Too conservative?

Had they simply skimmed it?

Or did they trust her analysis more than she trusted it herself?

By the time they stepped into Bailey's office, Taylor's nerves were steady but taut—the feeling before diving into cold water.

Bailey's First Reaction: Hope, Then Something Else

Bailey listened quietly, in the way that made everyone sit up a little straighter.

When Taylor finished, he tapped the cover page once.

"I appreciate how thoroughly you de-risked this," he said.

"It's clear you're thinking like owners. And the potential here… it's significant."

Taylor exhaled. For a heartbeat, she let herself feel proud.

Then Bailey flipped to the ROI chart.

"But let me ask," he said, voice even, "this 10x projection… what exactly is it built on?"

Taylor opened her mouth—then hesitated.

She'd followed the model. The assumptions were standard. The shape of the curve looked like every acceptable business case she'd studied.

Bailey waited.

"It assumes adoption beyond your department," she said. "And workflow changes. And… coordination with other groups."

"And training," Bailey added softly. "And process redesign. And political capital."

He wasn't reprimanding her.

He was surfacing the invisible.

Drew and Ira both shifted uncomfortably.

Bailey looked at all three of them.

"Let me be very direct," he said.

"If I approve this investment, the return won't come from Van's software. Or GenAI. Or data integration."

He paused, letting the air tighten.

"It will come from *you*."

Drew's brows knit. Ira straightened.

Taylor felt her pulse in her ears.

"ROI projections are numbers," Bailey continued.

"Returns are commitments."

He closed the folder.

"So let me ask you plainly:

Are you—the three of you—willing to personally commit to delivering this 10x return? Not theoretically. Not on paper. In practice."

Silence.

Not awkward—revealing.

Taylor's stomach knotted.

The model said 10x.

Her instincts did not.

If it were her money, would she bet on that curve?

She knew the answer.

Drew stared at the table. The personnel crisis, the missed client calls—she didn't have enough ground truth to stand behind this yet.

Ira breathed out slowly. "No," she said. "Not at that level. Not yet."

Taylor almost winced hearing it aloud.

Bailey nodded. "I appreciate the honesty."

Both Drew and Ira read the nod as a polite rejection.

It's Not a No

Bailey leaned forward.

"I'm not saying we shouldn't do this. I'm saying we shouldn't *pretend* we can deliver something we can't stand behind."

He pushed the proposal gently back toward them.

"Bring me a number you *believe* in. One you're willing to fight for when this gets hard—because it will."

"And don't give me a 10x number your project management course told you to write down. I'd rather fund something with a realistic return you'll fight to deliver than a number in a business case—an empty promise that gets put in a drawer and never comes out again."

The room stayed still.

"This is not about ambition," Bailey said. "It's about ownership."

As they left the office, Ira muttered, "We knew this was coming..." Drew rubbed her forehead, already scanning her calendar for where to wedge in client calls. But Taylor... felt something unexpected.

Not defeat. Not shame. Clarity.

Bailey hadn't shut the door.

He'd handed them the key—and asked them to prove they deserved to use it.

This is fair, she thought.

He isn't saying *no.*

He's saying: *show me you'll own what you promise.*

Rebuilding the Proposal—This Time With Agency

That night, Taylor rebuilt the business case from scratch.

No templates.

No assumptions borrowed from the course.
No curves she didn't believe in.
The new plan was grounded, specific, real:

- Three months to refine the model and measure actual performance gains.
- Nine months to roll it out to one pilot team and see what would be required to scale.
- Clear decision criteria.
- Roles defined.
- Risks acknowledged.
- And a minimum ROI projection of 1.2x over three years for the pilot alone.

Modest. Achievable. Owned.

At the end, she added a new page: A commitment statement for her, Drew, and Ira to sign.

The next morning, Drew read it twice.

"This…" she said quietly, "is something I can stand behind. Let me speak with those clients today."

Why Proof Beats Promise

In a firm like Vic Titious, change doesn't hinge on forecasts.

Or models. Or the elegance of a PowerPoint.

It hinges on proof:

- Proof that the problem is real.
- Proof that the solution works in the mess of everyday practice.

- Proof that the people leading the effort will not vanish when things get difficult.

Promises are cheap. Commitments should cost something.

And that cost—time, attention, ownership—is precisely what makes returns real.

That's why Bailey asked the only question that mattered:

What return are *you* willing to commit to?

Because committed leaders create committed teams. And committed teams deliver results a model can only try to predict.

Part 3 Summary: Developing Solutions

Turning a promising idea into a viable solution is rarely a straight line—especially when the future is moving as fast as GenAI and agentic workflows.

In this section, Taylor, Drew, Ira, and Van navigate the fuzzy front-end between inspiration and execution, encountering false starts, skeptical vendors, shifting priorities, and unexpected clarity.

Taylor learns that starting isn't the hard part—*staying focused, testing wisely, and adjusting intentionally* is.

Drew shifts from cautious gatekeeper to strategic sponsor once she sees the opportunities.

Ira balances pragmatism with experimentation.

And Bailey, to his credit, demands something many organizations shy away from: commitment, not just potential.

Innovation doesn't require certainty—it requires structure, shared ownership, and constant recalibration.

Key Takeaways

- **Recognize that false starts are normal.** Most innovation projects begin with more energy than clarity; structured discovery turns momentum into meaningful progress.
- **Treat pilots as structured experiments.** A good pilot tracks assumptions, tests key hypotheses, and leads to a deliberate decision.
- **Anchor progress in milestones, not master plans.** With GenAI and agentic workflows still evolving, discovery-driven planning keeps teams adaptive and focused on what matters most.

Reflection Questions

Think of an innovation project in your organization that started strong but lost momentum:

- Where did clarity or structure break down?
- Would the outcome have changed if key assumptions were tested early?

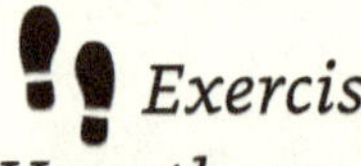

Exercise

Hypotheses Testing

Pick a current AI project and consider the following:

- What assumptions is your team making about users, clients, or value creation?

- In your context, what are your 'four databases + old pricing system' mess?
- Who plays the role of "Drew" in your project—the business sponsor? Are they being invited into the project early enough—or only expected to endorse it afterward?
- How often do you revisit project plans? Are updates driven by real learning—or are you sticking to old roadmaps despite changing conditions?

Going forward, define a pilot that:

- Tests one core assumption.
- Has a clear success threshold
- Ends with a go/no-go decision

A useful way to word the hypothesis you want to test is: If we [take a specific action], we expect to see [result] because [assumption]. We'll know it worked if [measurement].

"The real risk isn't asking. It's assuming we already know what our clients need—and finding out later that we were wrong."

Part 4
Pivots and Unexpected Turns

Groundwork and Growing Pains

The next three months were anything but smooth.

At Ira's suggestion, Taylor had begun hosting informal "brown bag" sessions to share early lessons from GenAI adoption and agentic workflow usage. Interest was real—but so was skepticism. Those who had taken the habit-building course were cautiously curious; holdouts were openly dismissive, warning about hype, erratic outputs, and headline risk—fearing GenAI could land Vic Titious in the wrong news story.

Despite a 40 percent increase in the use of GenAI, alignment was elusive. Some feared losing the value of their hard-won expertise. Others were frustrated by hits and misses. And yet, beneath the noise, Taylor sensed energy: not compliance, but engagement—messy, unpredictable, and real.

Her takeaway was sobering: if a simple training

sparked this much friction, scaling agentic workflows firmwide would demand more than enthusiasm. It would require proof, persistence, and a strategy to turn debate into momentum.

Navigating Uncertainty

The pilot with Van had shown what groundwork was required. Taylor spent hours alongside Ira's team—reviewing Application Programming Interface (API) docs, sitting through vendor demos, and cleaning up old files and folders. Ira raised flags almost daily: security gaps, brittle integrations. Progress was real, but painfully slow.

Meanwhile, Taylor still didn't have funding approval for the $200K Van was expecting. He had been pushing Vic Titious to make the purchase decision, since the software performed as expected. Taylor was not amused because when they set the pilot goals together, Van had pushed speed aside as something to figure out later. In hindsight, she understood why, since speed was a real and known issue, and as a result, their relationship had soured.

Drew still hadn't conducted the client interviews—a delay Taylor found increasingly frustrating. Together, it meant that while she was working day and night, there was still no formal approval beyond the initial $50K.

It made Taylor more than uncomfortable. A friend of hers had just been told that she had to look for another job. She, too, had taken on many "special" projects and was praised for all the extra work she had done. Yet, when the numbers were tight at the end of the year, her friend was the first who had been let go. Taylor could only hope that it would not happen to her, too. With Drew's reassurances, Taylor tried to brush things like that aside and focus on making progress, but that was not always easy.

If the technology would just work… but even that wasn't the case. The speed of the calculations remained the bottleneck. The results took forever to show up when pulling data from the full database. Van promised it could be solved but toggled between helpful and unavailable as he chased clients with committed budgets. Stitching messy, inconsistent data together fast enough to make it useful and affordable was the challenge. While she didn't want to admit it, she knew she still needed Van.

Then, one afternoon, Taylor tried a different pre-processing approach on a representative subset. The run finished in half the time, with 95.9 percent accuracy. Not perfect, but inside the threshold they'd set.

"We'll need to see what this means for the end result," Ira cautioned. "But… this could work."

Taylor logged the win and updated the project board. No champagne yet—but after three grueling months, it felt like a real breakthrough.

Sustaining Momentum

The next morning, Taylor's project management course unlocked its next module: Validate with End Users. It sounded obvious, but within Vic Titious, it wasn't.

She skimmed the first paragraph and felt a sense of recognition—as if someone had finally put words to what she'd been struggling to articulate.

"*In most professional service firms, client relationships are carefully stewarded by seasoned professionals. That's why the phrase 'let's talk to clients' can trigger hesitation. It's not about avoiding feedback—it's about protecting trust.*"

Taylor underlined the next sentence:

"*Waiting until things are polished can be costly. Early client feedback is your only true compass.*"

She scrolled further:

How to Approach Client Conversations:

- *Prepare—know what you want to learn.*
- *Clarify the purpose of the conversation upfront.*
- *Ask how they currently handle things—and why.*
- *Listen more than you talk.*
- *Capture insights—don't promise anything.*

Taylor smiled, as now she had something to bring to Drew—not just ask Drew if she'd done the interviews, but how to make them happen.

She waited for the right moment to bring up the client interviews once again.

Drew stiffened. "Client conversations?"

Taylor nodded. "We're not ready for that," Drew said

quickly. "We're still testing internally."

Taylor didn't argue—now she recognized the pattern. Drew would probably never feel "ready."

Just then, Bailey walked by and caught the tail end of their exchange. "How are things going?" he asked.

Taylor seized the opening, "We're debating whether to talk to a few clients about the recent findings."

Bailey nodded thoughtfully. "What's the goal?"

"To validate whether faster turnaround is something clients would actually value enough to pay for—or switch for." Taylor replied.

He studied them both. Drew looked tense; Taylor looked expectant. He knew this dance well. Client conversations were sacred territory. One poorly framed call could put years of trust on the line.

"You know," Bailey said gently, "I understand why you hesitate, Drew. It's not easy to ask for feedback early—but waiting will cost more than asking."

Neither spoke, but both were listening.

"What if someone from my team made these calls?" he continued. "Keep it light. Make it broader than just this project. A simple check-in: What are your top priorities this quarter? How are you implementing GenAI? What's changing for your clients? That kind of thing."

Drew crossed her arms. "Even then, what if they say yes—this is important? Are we supposed to take that at face value?"

Bailey smiled faintly. "No. That's where framing matters. The goal isn't to sell them something. It's to learn. We'll ask about their onboarding experience—what worked, what didn't. If they tell us, without prompting, that they'd value better forecasts, then we know it's real."

He glanced at Taylor. "And no, we don't ask for a financial commitment yet. But if they share it's a top priority and they're frustrated with the current process, that's worth hearing—before we sink more hours into building something they might not need."

Taylor nodded slowly, remembering the course module: *Plan, Frame, Listen. Capture insights—but don't promise anything.*

Bailey's tone shifted, firm now. "The real risk isn't asking. It's assuming we already know what our clients need—and finding out later that we were wrong."

Both could see Bailey was right.

The Message from the Market

Over the next two weeks, Taylor and a colleague from Bailey's team co-hosted five client calls. They kept the conversations broad—onboarding experiences, turnaround times, service quality, recurring bottlenecks, and what clients were exploring with GenAI.

Patterns emerged quickly: speed mattered. So did accuracy. And yes—GenAI was promising. But one conversation changed everything.

"We've been looking into automating forecasts ourselves," a client said. "Mainly to make outcomes more predictable."

Taylor leaned in. "You mean... the forecast analysis?"

"Exactly. Right now, we wait weeks for your forecast. And honestly? They're often off. We need those predictions before we act—not as a postscript."

Taylor felt the weight of that pause. Then the client added, almost casually:

"There's a Silicon Valley startup doing this already. They just raised ten million. Their pitch? "*Forecasts in 24 hours for $500.*"

Taylor kept her face neutral, but her pen froze mid-sentence. She wrote one word in the margin, underlined twice: Disruption.

Getting Disrupted

Drew had always been pragmatic. Skeptical, even. That was her role. While others chased shiny new tools, she stayed grounded—asking the hard questions: *How would this actually work? Who's responsible? What could go wrong?*

It was the same skepticism that had kept her from pushing on an early hunch—that improved forecasts could help to change their business model. She'd dismissed the idea at the time. Too many question marks. Too much to take on. Too risky to bring up without something concrete.

But now?

Now, she couldn't shake it.

The startup that had been mentioned during the

client interviews wasn't some half-baked idea. They had a real product. Real funding. It sent a clear message. And worst of all—they were targeting the exact part of the process Drew had identified as an area where Vic Titious was vulnerable and that needed improvement.

Automated forecasts. Delivered in 24 hours. For $500.

Taylor had said it so casually—*"They just raised ten million."*

Drew hadn't stopped thinking about it since.

That night, she stayed late. The office was quiet. Most of the lights were off. Her inbox was finally clear, but her mind wasn't.

Taylor's notes from the client calls were still open on her screen. A tab for the startup's website blinked in the background. She skimmed their headlines again. Their promises. Their pricing.

She leaned back and let the implications settle.

I was right and wrong about the forecasts, she thought. *They matter. They always have. But now others see it too—and they're moving faster than we are.*

That was the thing about disruption, she realized.

It never looked impressive at first.

In fact, it often looked... clumsy.

Rough edges. Shaky accuracy. Surface-level analysis that didn't come close to the nuance clients expected. It was easy—almost *comforting*—to dismiss. Drew wanted to tell herself the technology of the startup wasn't ready, that it couldn't possibly compete with the depth, experience, and polish of Vic Titious' expertise. It was exactly what she had done before she had tried ChatGPT for the first time.

And yet, underneath all the imperfections, the direction was clear. The pace of improvement. The potential scale. The inevitability.

It didn't take Drew much effort to see it: The startup's early results weren't perfect, but they were *good enough* to start raising eyebrows. And in another six months? A year? The very things that looked rough today might be automated, refined, or even productized.

Could Vic Titious wait—let themselves believe it wasn't real until it was polished, proven, and safe? No, Drew thought. If we wait, it might be too late. By the time we would be able to act, the startup would be trusted. Embedded. Growing. And Vic Titious would be the ones playing catch-up.

That was the unsettling part of disruption.

It didn't ask for permission. It wouldn't wait until Vic Titious was ready.

Drew glanced at her screen. She remembered Kodak—and her uncle's quiet bitterness when the layoffs came. Change wasn't just theory; it had consequences.

While it always seemed odd to her that Kodak shelved the digital camera they invented, she now started to understand how that could have happened. It was easy to convince yourself that the core business was strong enough to compete. Especially when their loyal clients—professional photographers—had agreed, until they didn't. She could already hear the arguments her colleagues would make:

- The startup's quality isn't there yet.
- Our clients aren't asking for cheaper forecasts.
- These reports are for smaller, less profitable clients.
- Nobody knows our clients like we do.

All true.

All dangerously comfortable excuses.

The seemingly safe choice, she realized, was to do nothing. Keep things as they were. Stick to high-end engagements. Keep forecasts bundled into the full-service package. After all, that was what Vic Titious was known for.

But Drew knew where that path led. Eventually, it wouldn't be safe, it wouldn't even be stagnant, it would lead to decay. Today, the firm still had a strong reputation. Today, they had funds to invest—smartly. Today, they had the relationships needed to get real feedback.

In a year? That window might be smaller. In five? It might be gone.

She opened a blank note and typed, slowly:

Keep serving today's clients.

Invest like our options are already shrinking because they are.

She stared at the line for a long time. Not panicking. Not abandoning what worked. But no longer pretending they had unlimited time.

A solution would not be easily found, she realized, and sitting behind her desk wouldn't get her any further. Perhaps a good night's sleep would help give her a fresh perspective.

Defining the Differentiator

By morning, Drew's resolve had hardened. The startup was fast—but speed wasn't everything. Vic Titious had assets the startup couldn't touch:

- Deep domain expertise
- A treasure trove of client-specific data
- Long-standing relationships and credibility

Still, Drew knew how this story usually ended. Firms waited too long—then scrambled:

- Buy the disruptor (and watch culture clash sink the deal)
- Start a pricing war (and burn cash for little gain)
- Dismiss the trend (until it was too late to catch up)

Not on her watch.

She grabbed a marker and faced the whiteboard. At the top, in bold strokes:

We don't beat them by being the same.

We beat them by being better at what they can't touch.

Below, her ideas took shape fast:

- Focus on accuracy and nuance—the startup will

cut corners; Vic Titious can't.

- Deliver insights, not just data—context is our edge.
- Automate the front end—but double down on implementation and advisory.
- Build workflows the startup can't replicate—powered by client data.

It wasn't a full strategy. But it was a framework—a way to go on offense.

Drew snapped a photo. No more tweaking. It was time to test assumptions. Taylor could help shape the plan. Ira would stress-test the tech. But this wasn't just alignment. It was a pivot.

And for that, she needed Bailey.

Changing Direction

Later that morning, Drew walked into Bailey's office. He looked up with a curious smile. "Everything okay?"

"I think we need to shift the plan," Drew said.

Bailey raised an eyebrow.

"Not abandon it," she added quickly. "But aim higher. Much higher."

She placed her phone on the table, the photo of her whiteboard on the screen.

"I don't think the startup's the threat we thought it was. But I do think they're the signal. We've been playing it safe—just trying to catch up. What if we didn't do that?"

She paused.

"What if we led instead?"

Bailey leaned forward, scanning the whiteboard photo on her phone. He didn't speak right away.

"Lead how?" he asked eventually, his tone even.

"By focusing on what the startup can't replicate," Drew said. "We're never going to outrun this startup on speed or a slick user interface. But we know our clients. We can automate just enough to move faster—then double down on accuracy, nuance, and results our clients can actually act on."

Bailey nodded slowly, but his expression stayed cautious.

"I'm not saying we blow up the project," Drew continued. "The foundation is solid. But the target needs to shift. We're not just proving a tool that works and saves my team time. We should be validating a new kind of offering—insight-led and offered for a fixed-fee."

He exhaled. "That's a big swing."

"I know," she said. "But the signals are clear. If we wait until the startup has polished its offering, we'll be too late. I'm not asking for full commitment—just permission to explore this direction. If it doesn't hold up, we walk it back."

Bailey looked out the window, then back at her.

"You'll need to bring the team in on this."

"I will," Drew said. "But before I do, I need to know if you back this shift. At least enough to test it."

He gave a short nod. "Okay. You've got room to run.

Bring Ira in, loop in Taylor—and show me something I can take to the board that's grounded in client value, not just internal momentum."

Drew smiled. "That's exactly the plan."

Knowing How Will Become a Commodity

GenAI isn't just improving—it's accelerating beyond human speed. Recent GenAI models have already outperformed experts on complex reasoning tasks and standardized tests, and systems like AlphaGo have mastered games once thought impossible for machines. In this arms race, "knowing how" to draft a contract, analyze data, or write code will no longer differentiate you.

It becomes a commodity.

What remains valuable?

- Acting on insights before competitors do
- Helping clients move from "now what?" to "we've got this"
- Turning forecasts into results—not just numbers
- Leading change in complex, human systems

GenAI can predict outcomes at lightning speed, but it can't navigate politics, build trust, or make change happen. Those who master these skills will win—not by knowing more, but by acting faster and smarter.

A Shift in the Project Goals

Ira listened carefully as Drew laid out her thoughts.

She didn't bring a full proposal—just the whiteboard sketch: ideas about automation, differentiation, and building something competitors couldn't easily copy. It wasn't too different from what the team had been working on, but Drew was more explicit about where the real value would lie—not in saving time for her department or producing forecasts, but in turning these insights into faster, fixed-fee solutions that clients could act on.

Ira nodded, absorbing the shift. No questions about why. No challenge on risk. Just:

"Have you shared this with Taylor yet—or do you want me to help tighten it first?"

"Not yet and yes," Drew said. "I only talked to Bailey—to get his buy-in."

The next morning, Drew called the team together.

"We're not walking away from the project," she began. "We're building on it. But it's time to recalibrate."

Taylor looked up, wary. "You mean expand the scope?"

"Yes," Drew said evenly. "Slightly. But this isn't a distraction—it's where the value is."

She walked them through the signals: pilot results, client conversations, and the startup looming in the background.

"Automated forecasting isn't the problem," she said.

"It's the opportunity. Clients aren't asking for cheaper forecasts—they're asking for predictability. If we can deliver that through fixed fees and faster service, we differentiate."

Bailey leaned back, thoughtful. He'd understood the strategic hint before. Now they were talking implementation. And he knew how easily a pivot could look like drift.

"I get the logic," he said finally. "But the board will see this as scope creep. That'll trigger red flags."

Drew nodded. "I'm not asking for a blank check. Just space to validate whether this direction holds water. If it does, we go to the board with evidence—not theory."

Bailey studied her, then glanced at Taylor, who had been quiet.

"Taylor?"

She met his gaze, steady but cautious. "I want this to succeed. I've put a lot into it already. But if we're adding scope and visibility, I need clarity on my role. Not a title—just a formal commitment."

Silence. Then Drew nodded in support. "Fair enough," Bailey said. "We'll sort that out. For now—can I count on you to keep leading?"

Taylor exhaled. "Yes. Absolutely."

Bailey stood. "Bring me something crisp for the board. And don't lose momentum. They're watching—and expecting something big."

He paused at the door.

"If we're making this pivot—let's stick the landing."

Navigating the Shift

Taylor reread Drew's notes. The plan was bold, sweeping—and, if she was honest, terrifying. Drew saw the disruption clearly and seemed certain about what needed to happen. Taylor wasn't. That was why she'd pushed back. She was still surprised by Drew's reaction—affirming, even—but now she was committed.

Committed to what, exactly? The question gnawed at her.

Something about this new direction felt… off. Not wrong, but unmoored. As if they were suddenly running a different race on a track she didn't recognize.

Was this scope creep?

Or simply how innovation projects behaved when the world shifted under their feet?

She didn't know.

But she knew someone who might—and whom she had been avoiding.

Van.

He was still in the dark.

He didn't know she'd found ways to make the forecasting faster. He didn't know about the startup. He didn't know that Vic Titious was now reconsidering the whole project direction.

And Taylor herself kept circling the same question: *Why not just use the startup's technology? It's $500—far cheaper than Van.*

She decided to call him.

His phone rang for a long time before he finally picked up.

"Taylor! Hey," Van said, upbeat in that salesman-on-autopilot way. "What's up?"

She could hear he wasn't expecting much from her anymore—and why would he?

So she decided to go in cold.

"A lot has happened since we last talked."

"Oh… good or bad?" he asked cautiously.

"Complicated," she replied. "Have you heard of this startup doing predictions for $500? They're well-funded."

A pause.

"Of course," Van said, recovering quickly. "Them. Yes. I know them."

He absolutely did not.

"I've been following them closely," he added, confidence plastered over panic. "What about them?"

"They're disrupting us," Taylor said gently. "And our project. They can do in minutes what takes us… well, much longer."

Another pause—sharper this time.

"I see," he said quietly. "Maybe this is better discussed in person. We've not seen each other for a long time, and… look, do you have any plans for tonight or tomorrow?"

He needed time to look up this startup.

Taylor needed perspective beyond her own and Drew's.

"Tonight's fine," she said.

Moving Forward Together

Van arrived late, clearly rushed, wearing the expression of someone blindsided but determined not to show it. He smoothed his shirt, forcing a confident smile.

"Alright," he said, settling into the seat. "Let's pick up where we left off. You said this startup is fast. And loud. But loud doesn't always mean good."

Taylor didn't respond right away. She just watched him.

That unsettled him more than he expected.

He cleared his throat. "Look, I've seen startups come and go. Half of them flame out before they ship anything real."

Taylor raised an eyebrow. Not confrontational—just waiting for him to get to the point.

"But," he continued, adjusting, "I can see why Vic Titious is paying attention. And why you're concerned."

Van swallowed.

She wasn't attacking him, but she wasn't rescuing him either.

That caught him off guard.

"So," he said, shifting into a tone that sounded almost collaborative, "tell me what you're thinking. What's Drew planning?"

Taylor leaned forward, steady and composed. "This startup is cheap and fast. Which means that even if we hit our cost-savings target, the client might still switch to them. I considered using their tech ourselves, but data-security-wise that is probably not a good idea."

"Understandable… smart thinking," Van replied, nodding slowly. He kept his tone neutral, but internally he was doing math he hoped didn't show on his face. If this client could switch because of speed or price… others could too.

"Drew thinks we need a pivot," Taylor continued. "Not copying the startup—but going beyond their offering. What she's proposing is massive. I'm not convinced it makes the project better. Maybe just bigger."

Van tapped the table lightly, buying time. He needed to stay helpful. He needed to find a way to stay relevant.

"Look," he said, lifting his chin slightly, "scope creep is when a project gets sloppy—when people add things because they can't say no. That doesn't seem to be what's happening here."

Taylor tilted her head, listening.

"This is responding to new information," he said. "If the environment changes, sticking to the original blueprint just to feel in control… that's actually the bigger risk."

This part was honest.

Everything around it was strategically phrased.

Taylor considered his response. She didn't give him the satisfaction of immediate agreement.

"So," she said, "what are you suggesting?"

For a moment, Van's old defensiveness flickered in his eyes. Then he let out a small breath—measured, careful.

"I'm suggesting we work together," he said. "No posturing. No friction. If Drew is right, and there's a smarter way to approach this, I can help. I want to help. We're on the same side here."

Taylor held his gaze.

She could sense he wasn't telling her everything—he never did—but he was offering something real enough.

"Alright," she said. "If we're collaborating, I need execution. Not selling. No pressure. Actual partnership."

Van nodded, the gesture small but unmistakably sincere. "Fair. Let's go over the options."

Taylor didn't smile, but she felt steadier than she had in days.

"Good," she said. And together they discussed the moves that would be smart to make in the next weeks and months. Moves that would help Taylor give direction to Drew's new plans.

When they stepped out of the bar, Taylor didn't feel a dramatic revelation—just clarity. A direction emerging through the noise.

This isn't scope creep, she thought.

It's adaptive innovation.

It was more responsibility than she'd bargained for. But now that Van had skin in the game—she didn't have to carry it alone.

Regaining Control

Taylor knew she needed to steady the project. Van was back in the mix, but she didn't want to lean on him too heavily.

Her project management course offered a way forward: milestone-driven planning—flexible, but structured enough to keep control.

Later that week, she sat down with Drew and Ira to walk through Van's proposed approach and how collaboration would work.

"Instead of a full roadmap," Taylor explained, "we set high-level goals for the next 30 to 90 days—clear milestones, assumptions to test, and room to adapt as we learn."

Drew nodded slowly.

"I like that," she said. "Flexible—but accountable."

Realigning the Path

By week's end, Taylor had reframed the project around new goals—grounded, but still ambitious:

Short term: Complete the onboarding tool everyone agreed was essential. Target >95 percent accuracy with five-minute latency—far from perfect, but acceptable for internal use.

Medium term: Convert manual prediction reports into automated forecasts with a feedback loop—at least as accurate as the startup's offering. Ideally, build in-house with Van to avoid exposing proprietary data. Embed forecasts into onboarding and use them to offer fixed-fee solutions.

Long term: Position Vic Titious as the go-to firm for the full trajectory—from strategy to execution.

Not just insights (as the startup promised). Not just implementation (as they were known for). Both: integrated and differentiated.

Taylor revisited the business case using the reverse income statement method. The plan wasn't audacious, but it was solid:

- Target outcome: $500K annual revenue, 40 percent margin, within two years.
- Cost envelope: No more than $900K over the same period.
- Staged investment:
  • $200K now for the Minimum Viable Solution and pilot with select clients
  • $400K next year for department rollout (contingent on pilot success)
  • $300K later for firmwide scaling

Client interviews suggested the revenue assumption was realistic. Taylor documented key uncertainties—pricing, adoption, conversion—to ensure decisions stayed evidence-based, not optimism-driven.

When she presented the updated plan, Bailey invited the team to lunch. After the plates arrived, he raised his glass.

"Look," he said, "I know we're not done. Not even close. I still need board approval. But don't lose sight of how far we've come."

He glanced around the table.

"Six months ago, none of this existed. Now we have

a plan—built on client feedback—with a strategy to go head-to-head with a VC-backed startup."

His tone shifted.

"You're the engine. But don't forget to connect the rest of the train. As you saw in the brown bag sessions, not everyone in the firm is on board yet. And clients aren't fully there either."

He smiled.

"So keep moving—and keep bringing others along in small steps. For today, let's acknowledge how far we've gotten and what you've learned. That's real progress."

Everyone smiled—including Drew.

RISE: Building Momentum on Purpose

The glow from lunch faded fast. Taylor stared at her screen, unease creeping in. The stakes were growing. The risks were real. And the board still hadn't approved a dime beyond the initial pilot. How long could she keep Van engaged without a formal commitment?

She needed more than a to-do list. She needed clarity. That's when she remembered something Bailey had mentioned: the RISE framework.

Return. Invest. Support. Expectations

Maybe this could anchor the next sprint—not just to guide tasks, but shape the thinking behind them.

Using RISE to Plan the Next Sprint

Instead of diving into execution, Taylor framed the sprint around four questions:

- Return: What result will we deliver in the next 90 days?
- Invest: What time, support, and people will we commit?
- Support: What access, training, or approvals will we need?
- Expectations: What learning will we capture—even if the outcome shifts?

She then mapped it out:

- Return: Feedback from five clients on the minimum viable solution —focused on value, not a demo.
- Invest: Taylor as project manager (20 hours/ week), Drew reconnecting with clients (~5 hours), Ira's team providing integration support (~30 hours), together representing a substantial, time-bound investment over the next 90 days.
- Support: Collaborate with Van for the solution build; formalizing Taylor's role; Bailey and Drew to field internal questions.
- Expectations: Client validation as the decision criterion. If interest and willingness to pay are clear, board approval of the $200K investment is triggered.

Taylor gave the project a name: **Project Polaris**—a North Star for clarity in uncharted territory. When she hit *Save* on the updated board presentation, the plan still wasn't perfect. The risks were real. But for the first time, momentum felt deliberate—not accidental.

Pre-Mortem: Facing Failure Before It Happens

Her course materials suggested one more technique she wanted to try: a pre-mortem. It was meant to flip the question. Instead of asking, *"What will make this succeed?"* ask: *"Imagine it's six months after launch. The project failed completely. Why?"*

Taylor opened Copilot and typed: "Can you do a pre-mortem on this project plan?" The results came back fast—and sobering:

If Project Polaris has failed six months from now, here's why:

- Vic Titious' reputation as a fee-for-service firm—the shift to fixed fees felt like old wine in a new bottle.
- Clients were unsure if the new offer was worth paying for—differentiation was unclear.
- Internal systems were not ready for scaled integration.
- Legal flagged unacceptable risks tied to fixed fees.
- Unexpected resistance arose among junior staff—fearing GenAI would kill their billable hours.

The last line stopped her cold. This wasn't just about tech. It was about people—people like her. If this failed, she might be first in line for cuts.

Taylor immediately knew that it was not just about her, but also about all those who joined the firm around the same time. This project would replace the work she used to do too.

She stared at the screen.

She took a deep breath. If it didn't work, she'd lose

But if it did? She'd be the one who made it possible.

And then, unexpectedly, a thought hit her—football. A sport she'd never cared about beyond the roar of the stadium crowd. She had never understood how athletes could train so hard, knowing every play meant being slammed to the ground, every tackle a potential career-ender.

Now she did.

What she was doing wasn't so different—hitting wall after wall, getting knocked down by setbacks, and still getting up. Not for the guarantee of victory, but for the thrill of the fight. For the rush of clearing each obstacle.

If it were only about the end result, she would have quit long ago. She realized something else: she loved the process. The learning. The grit. The climb. That alone was enough to keep going—because the reward wasn't just the win. It was becoming the kind of leader who could take the hits and still move forward.

The Board's Cold Water

A few weeks later, Bailey walked into the quarterly board meeting with confidence. The pilot had shown promising results. Van was collaborating. Client feedback on the new plans was strong. Taylor had pulled the numbers together, and they looked solid.

He was ready to present the bold idea they'd asked for. He'd prepared for questions about timelines, implementation—even security.

What he hadn't prepared for was the ice-cold reception to the $900K investment proposal.

"Sounds like scope creep to me," said Margaret, the firm's longest-serving partner. "What happens when every other department wants similar investments?" added Thomas, arms folded, leaning back in his chair. Another voice cut in: "Isn't our reputation built on custom, high-touch service? What message does fixed-fee automation send to our clients?"

Within ten minutes, Bailey's grand vision had unraveled into uncomfortable silence and skeptical stares.

And then it hit him: these weren't just financial objections. They were the same fears Taylor had surfaced in her pre-mortem:

- Automation might cheapen the brand
- The firm wasn't ready for scaled integration
- Fixed fees carried untested risks
- Junior staff would fear for their jobs and professional development

- And the $500K annual revenue could take years to materialize

The board wasn't being reckless—they had a point. No signed clients. Only interest.

Bailey felt the air tighten. This bold idea—the one the board had asked for—was slipping away. And he knew something they didn't: momentum was fragile. Kill it now, and the opportunity would never return.

The $900K wasn't a blank check. It was a staged plan. $200K now to build out the minimum viable solution. $400K next year for rollout. $300K later for scale. But the headline number was all they heard.

Walking out of the boardroom, Bailey understood something he hadn't fully grasped going into the meeting. The numbers weren't the real problem. Their firm structure was.

Vic Titious, like most professional service firms, was a partnership—a loose confederation of practices tied together by an annual profit-sharing agreement. A model that had proven its value through time, but now, Bailey realized, it would stand in the way of bold innovation bets because partners expected one of two things:

- A direct benefit to their corner of the business
- Or a return within the same fiscal year, so the investment wouldn't put a dent in their compensation

Fifty thousand? Even two hundred? Easy. But nine hundred? That changed the conversation. It raised questions about fairness, equity, and opportunity cost.

And in the GenAI era, that was the real risk—not the technology, not the startup, but a governance model built for yesterday's world.

Bailey exhaled. The future wasn't waiting—and neither could he. He needed a bridge. Something to keep this project alive and get board approval.

Ira's Strategic Insight

"I've been where you are," Ira said as Bailey leaned against her doorframe after the board meeting.

"The board shot down my infrastructure proposal twice before I figured out how to frame it."

She leaned forward, her tone shifting from sympathetic to strategic.

"The brown bag sessions have been working. People are curious. What if Taylor and Drew wrote up a white paper about the onboarding workflow—something clear, professional—and tracked downloads among clients to gauge interest?"

Bailey looked up.

"Then," she continued, "invite the most engaged clients to a small roundtable. Make it exploratory. Not a pitch."

Bailey raised an eyebrow. "And then?"

"At the end, ask who'd be willing to participate in a pilot. Even if it's not fully funded or 100 percent automated and a slimmed-down version of what we could do, it would provide forward motion. Show traction. And give the board something tangible—proof that clients will pay."

It won't cover the full $200K needed to build out the solution and Taylor would still have to do most of the analyses manually. But if we can get commitment for say $15K for a few pilots each, it would show the board that there is a *there* there.

And maybe, Bailey thought, that's what the board really needed—not promises, but proof. No guarantees on the $500K new revenue, but just enough evidence to believe it was safe to keep moving forward.

Part 4 Summary

- Over several tumultuous months, Taylor and her team navigated setbacks, delays, and internal friction while trying to turn a promising GenAI pilot into a viable solution. Despite lacking formal funding, Taylor pushed forward—balancing technical hurdles, management hesitations, and fears about job security.
- Client conversations revealed both interest and a looming threat: a well-funded startup promising forecasts in 24 hours for $500. That signal forced Drew to pivot—shifting the project from incremental time savings to a bold new play: proactive, fixed-fee insights. What looked like scope creep became adaptive innovation,

anchored by milestone-driven planning and the RISE framework.

- But the board balked at a $900K investment. Their objections weren't just financial—they were cultural. In a partnership model built for stability, big bets feel risky. Ira's insight offered a lifeline: prove demand first through a white paper, client roundtable, and paid micro-pilots.
- The lesson? In the GenAI era, success doesn't hinge on perfection—it hinges on building just enough evidence to keep moving forward.

Key Takeaways

- Innovation rarely follows a straight line. Adaptation isn't failure—it's how progress happens.
- Scope creep dilutes value. Adaptive innovation sharpens focus through intentional learning.
- The RISE framework helps align efforts, expectations, and resources—especially in uncertain environments.
- Pre-mortems surface hidden risks early—before they quietly derail progress.
- When boards push back, it's often about fear, fairness, or identity—not just the budget.

Reflection Questions

- Think of a recent GenAI project or pilot that changed direction. Was it guided by new insight—

or by internal confusion and indecision?

- When your team pivots, do you communicate why—and what success looks like next?
- How do leaders in your organization typically respond to uncertainty: with caution, curiosity, or control?
- Are client conversations a regular practice—or something reserved for "later?"
- How would your board or leadership team respond to a bold investment without guaranteed ROI? What evidence would make them comfortable moving forward?

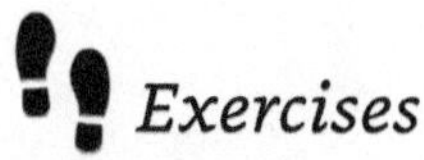

Exercises

Exercise 1: Craft a RISE-Aligned Plan

Choose a current or upcoming AI initiative and outline the following:

- **Return**—What does success look like in the next 30–90 days
- **Invest**—Who is committing time, energy, or resources?
- **Support**—What access, help, or approvals are required
- **Expectations**—What learning will happen, even if the outcome changes

Exercise 2: Run a Pre-Mortem

A **pre-mortem** helps you surface risks before they derail your project—not after. Unlike a post-mortem (which analyzes failure after the fact), a pre-mortem asks you to *imagine* failure in advance, so you can take action while there's still time.

Step-by-step:

1. **Set the scene**

   Imagine it is one year from now. Your project has completely failed. The results were disappointing. The initiative either stalled or was quietly abandoned.

2. **Ask yourself (or your team):**

- What went wrong?
- What warning signs did we ignore?
- What assumptions proved false?
- What internal resistance slowed us down?
- What external forces blindsided us?
- Who wasn't truly on board—and why?

3. **List 3–5 reasons the project failed.**
   Be honest. Be specific.
4. **For each risk, identify one action you could take now** to reduce the likelihood or impact of that failure scenario.

Optional Tip:

Turn the pre-mortem into a group exercise. Have each person write their own "failure story" in silence before sharing. The diversity of fears and insights is often surprising—and invaluable.

She suddenly understood why trust—not accuracy—was the real currency they were trading in

Part 5
Delivering Value and ROI

Underselling

Drew didn't look impressed when she heard the plan.

"You want me to sell $15K pilots," she said slowly, "to clients who are used to paying ten times that?" She shook her head. "Selling these client pilots will take as much time as delivering them. Probably more. And for what?"

It wasn't just skepticism. It was pragmatism mixed with pride. Ever since the first GenAI workshop, Drew had been wrestling with an uncomfortable truth: GenAI was eroding the value of the knowledge she'd spent decades mastering. What once required hours of careful research and expert judgment could now be approximated—badly, but fast—with a single prompt.

And while she had pushed for the bolder approach, she sometimes wished there was a way back. She didn't say it out loud, but this whole project felt like a precursor to the decay of value.

She felt like she was being asked to stop making

mille-feuille as a pastry chef and start selling cupcakes from a box mix.

Same kitchen. Same tools. Totally different outcome.

And now, not only was she expected to embrace the cake mix—she was supposed to price it like a bake sale.

"Why not just give them away?" she said. "At least then I'm not pretending this is a real offer."

It wasn't a tantrum. It was the honest frustration of someone who had built a career on nuance, depth, and judgment—now being asked to sell what felt thin, even disposable.

A Pause, and a Realization

The room fell quiet.

Drew leaned back in her chair, her expression guarded. But inside, her mind was racing. She knew there was no way back. The competition from the startup was real.

And she knew it because she'd tested it herself—drafting summaries, generating outlines, even modeling client forecasts. Some results were flawed. But most? Disturbingly good.

One quiet afternoon, she'd asked Copilot to analyze a real client dataset. The forecast wasn't perfect. But it was… acceptable. Maybe even sufficient.

That was the gut punch.

Clients wouldn't need Vic Titious the way they used to. Not for hours of bespoke analysis.

Flipping through the updated business case, Drew saw something else:

- The vision hadn't changed.
- The opportunity was still real.
- Clients still needed better onboarding.
- They just needed it delivered differently.

She closed her notebook and looked up.

Right.

The cake mix wasn't the point. The result—and the experience—were.

Clients weren't buying automation. They were buying faster delivery, predictable pricing, and peace of mind.

Still, the $15K price tag didn't sit well with her.

Taylor's New Challenge

Bailey broke the silence.

"I get it," he said gently. "This feels like a downgrade. You've spent years selling high-stakes strategy. Now it looks like we're shrinking what you do down to a test case."

He paused. "And for the record—I don't like the idea of doing these pilots for free. That would signal zero value. Clients wouldn't take them seriously, and we'd waste time and money without getting a meaningful signal back."

Bailey leaned forward. "So let's take a step back. Are we still aligned on the bigger picture? Do the strategy and commitments in the business case still hold?"

Drew stayed quiet, but didn't argue.

Bailey continued, his tone steady. "Remember why we built the business case. It wasn't about spreadsheets—it was about alignment. Without it, we'd have no yardstick when priorities shift or things get tough."

He ticked off the essentials:

- The problem: It started with efficiency gains. Now, it's survival—competing with a well-funded startup.
- Success: Not just 10 percent improvement. It's keeping clients happy and margins healthy.
- Timeline: Use the next 90 days to gather evidence and prove the business viability of the new solution.
- De-risking: We need to know if and what clients are willing to pay for our forecasting solution
- Next steps: Identify clients who need these forecasts and test their willingness to pay for pilots.
- Exit conditions: If clients won't pay more than the startup's pricing, we pull the plug.

Bailey looked around the room. "A strong business case isn't bureaucracy. It's our safety net. It makes sure we know what matters—so when the pressure hits, we have clarity. We need to know how to make trade-off decisions that impact our reputation, our margins, and our relationships."

He let the words settle, then asked, "Are you still aligned with these objectives?"

The room went quiet as everyone weighed the implications. Taylor's heart skipped a beat. Her entire future at the firm felt like it hung on this moment.

Bailey leaned in, more explicit now: "Are we still committed to making this work?"

One by one, heads nodded yes.

A New Path Forward

Bailey leaned forward. "Okay. Good to know we are all still aligned. Now, how do we make these pilots happen?"

He turned to Drew. "What if it's not your name on them?"

That got her attention.

"Taylor could lead the effort," Bailey said. "She's not tied to current relationships—so no risk of cannibalizing your work. She could target prospects who fit the ideal profile but aren't clients yet."

Drew considered it. Taylor had been committed, thoughtful, persistent. She understood the offering. She believed in it.

Still, Drew hesitated. "New clients are harder. No trust bank to draw from."

"True," Bailey nodded. "But no baggage either. No expectations to manage. A clean slate."

He turned to Taylor. "Are you up for that?"

Taylor hesitated. "Honestly? I am willing to give it a try. But I've never done sales before. It will be another mountain for me to climb."

Drew gave a small nod of respect. Taylor had poured her soul into this project. It was clear she was willing to do anything to turn it into a success, but that didn't mean it was fair to send her out alone.

"Taylor can't do this by herself," Drew said.

"She won't have to," Bailey replied. "We'll make sure she will get the sales support she needs."

And just like that, the plan shifted: Taylor would lead client acquisition—targeting new prospects. Harder, yes. But it would prove whether this new direction had legs.

The Startup Reality Check

Three weeks into the client pilot sales process, Taylor ran into her first real gut check.

During a call with a prospective client—one she'd been carefully nurturing—the conversation took a turn.

"We've been exploring options to increase the predictability of outcomes," the client said. "One thing we're evaluating is whether GenAI could speed up early analysis. Forecasts, in particular."

Taylor nodded. "We've been hearing that too. That is a known pain point."

The client leaned in. "So if your workflow helps pull together structured data faster—why wouldn't it be able to generate those forecasts automatically?"

Taylor took a breath. "You mean the first-level analysis? We've been experimenting. It's promising, but not bulletproof. And context still matters—especially for nuanced or high-risk cases."

The client smiled politely. "Sure. But there's this startup out of Silicon Valley that claims otherwise. They recently raised ten million. Their pitch is: *'"Forecasts in 24 hours for $500.'* Have you heard of them?"

She had.

Taylor had been tracking this startup closely ever since she heard of them.

But hearing it from a client—as a point of direct comparison—hit differently.

$500 vs. $15,000.

Fully automated vs. guided.

Tech-first vs. problem-first.

The competition wasn't hypothetical anymore. It was real.

Taylor sat with the tension. This wasn't about being *first*. It was about being *right*—delivering a solution that mattered to their clients.

She had to find the words to articulate the difference: Why Vic Titious didn't just offer faster reports—but deeper insight and a solution.

Why this wasn't a feature war—it was a workflow shift.

And why clients who cared about trust, context, and long-term results shouldn't settle for a $500 forecast that no one would stand behind.

Their client's CFO leaned back. "So help me understand—why should we pay you thirty times more than the startup down the street?" His tone was calm, but the implication hung heavy. It was on Taylor to defend Vic Titious.

Taylor felt the urge to rattle off Vic Titious' features—the richer dashboards, tighter integrations. She stopped herself. This wasn't about features. It was about consequences. About who would take responsibility when the answers were challenged.

So she reframed. "What we offer isn't just speed—it's accountability. We don't hand you numbers and disappear. We help you explain them, defend them, and act on them. That's the difference between a report and a solution."

Silence again—but now with nods of approval instead of skepticism. The conversation shifted from cost to confidence, from speed to outcomes.

The Trust Crisis

Taylor pulled it off. The client signed on for a $15K pilot—despite knowing about the $500 startup alternative.

She had explained the difference clearly: Vic Titious offered context, nuance, and a workflow that made the forecast actionable—not just automated.

The client had nodded. They got it. Or at least, she thought they had.

But now, a week later, Taylor sat staring at the first forecast output—and her stomach clenched.

It wasn't wrong. But it wasn't 100 percent right either.

Assumptions were baked into the model. Estimates that made sense in context—but could be misinterpreted if someone took the numbers at face value. And this client?

They had said they wanted speed—but what they really needed was certainty. Taylor reread the summary, then reread it again.

Her real fear wasn't that the output was bad—it was that it would be treated as flawless.

Before GenAI, no one expected perfection from a consultant's report. The PowerPoint was a jumping-off point—a tool for discussion.

But now? The numbers were *system-generated.* They looked final. Authoritative.

Which made every error feel riskier and every nuance harder to explain.

That was the dark irony of agentic workflows. They were designed to help people act faster and make better decisions. But they made people *afraid* to act at all—unless the machine was flawless.

And that standard? It didn't exist. At least not while using GenAI.

Taylor closed her laptop slowly.

She didn't doubt the value of the pilot results. But she suddenly understood why trust—not accuracy—was the currency they were trading in.

Trust meant the client could rely on her team to say when the model was wrong—and to stand behind it when it was right.

It meant surfacing assumptions instead of hiding them, so leaders could judge the risk for themselves.

It meant reframing "the answer" as the *start* of a conversation, not the end of one.

GenAI couldn't give certainty. But it could give options and leverage—if someone was willing to translate, interpret, and own the results.

That was the promise she had sold. And now, it was the standard she had to live up to.

A Loss and a Breakthrough Insight

Lying awake, Taylor pictured the client in their management meeting. The slide deck opening. Neat graphs on the screen. The client's CFO presenting the numbers with smooth certainty. Then the inevitable question: *"Where did this come from?"*

Would this client know how to explain the assumptions? The caveats? Should she admit the steps that were still manual? Or should she bluff—presenting the number as though it had come down from a sophisticated model based on Van's firm's technology, with the risk of it being seen as flawless and final?

That was the problem with agentic workflows built on probabilistic outcomes. The output looked like the truth, when in fact it was judgment in disguise. Useful, directional, but never absolute. And in the wrong hands—

or without the right framing—that difference could kill adoption.

That was why Taylor couldn't sleep. The work was better than before. But "better" no longer felt good enough.

The next day, after presenting the results, the unease deepened.

Taylor realized that, in part, the problem was that the output looked clean. Too clean. The client hadn't asked any questions. They'd nodded, thanked her, and said they'd get back to her.

But Taylor knew that look: The nods were too quick, the smiles too practiced. Polite uncertainty.

They didn't trust it. Not because the forecast was wrong, but because they didn't know how it was made. They couldn't see the work behind the numbers. There was no human they could hold accountable. No judgment they could probe.

She had promised nuance—but delivered a number.

On her way home, Taylor messaged Drew. "Can we talk? Something's not sitting right."

Hours later, in a small conference room, Taylor recapped the experience. Drew frowned. "But isn't that what they paid for?"

Taylor shook her head. "That's what they thought they wanted. But if we sell forecasts, we won't be any different than the startup—and will end up chasing speed over trust."

Drew listened quietly, then walked to the whiteboard.

"I've been thinking the same thing," she said. "It's what bothered me from the start." She wrote in big letters:

NOT SELLING FORECASTS

"We're selling outcomes," Drew continued. "The forecast is just the means. What clients want is certainty that something will *work*. That their decision will pay off."

She flipped through a few client files.

"Remember this one?" She tapped a folder. "They paid us $195,000 last quarter. Took our recommendation. Implemented the changes. Saw a 15 percent gain in efficiency."

Taylor nodded.

"What if we sold *that*?" Drew said. "The outcome—as the next step. Show them that we trust our numbers enough to act on it."

Taylor frowned. "You mean… like also offer the implementation, for a fixed fee?"

"Yes. A fixed-fee and outcome-based solution—like we mean it. We guarantee the result. We deliver the outcome we promise, or we don't get paid."

They both sat in silence, pondering their options.

"That's risky," Taylor said at last.

"It is," Drew agreed. "But it's a calculated risk. We already have the data. We already have the models. And now, we have the tech to predict better, deliver faster, and execute more consistently."

Drew looked at Taylor. "If clients are already

comparing us to $500 one-click startups, we can't win by being *slightly better.* We have to stand for something completely different."

The Business Model Shift

What Drew proposed wasn't a pricing tweak—it was a fundamental change in what Vic Titious offered:

Before:

- Sell time and expertise
- The client bears the risk.
- Success = hours worked

After:

- Sell guaranteed results
- Vic Titious bears the risk—but can manage it across projects.
- Success = measurable outcomes

It was bold. And exactly what Vic Titious' clients needed to justify higher fees in an AI-saturated world.

Their clients didn't want predictions—they wanted predictable results and a party they could hold accountable for the implementation.

And that was where GenAI changed everything.

Not because it was flawless—it wasn't, isn't, and never would be. The outputs remained probabilistic, messy at the edges, and still prone to error if taken at face value. But precisely because GenAI wasn't perfect, the role of Vic Titious became clearer.

The firm's value wasn't in producing a number. It was in translating that number into action. In exposing the assumptions instead of hiding them. And in building workflows where a probabilistic forecast could be turned into a reliable outcome.

GenAI gave them the speed to test more scenarios, the breadth to catch risks earlier, and the visibility to track progress in real time. But it was their judgment—and their willingness to stand behind the result—that would turn those machine outputs into client trust.

The startup sold a forecast.

Vic Titious could sell results—if they had the courage to own their forecasts.

Building Trust through Transparency

Taylor knew what she had to do next.

The first pilot had been a wake-up call. The client had nodded along, asked no questions—and then never followed up after the results presentation. A slick pitch, she'd learned the hard way, didn't build confidence.

So, for the next meeting, she redesigned her client pitch to:

- Confirm the client's challenges upfront.
- Walk through the data inputs and assumptions.
- Show how the system processed the information.
- Include confidence intervals and uncertainty ranges.
- Flag where human judgment still mattered—and

why.

"I'm not trying to impress you with magic," she told the next prospect.

"I'm trying to show you exactly how we reach our conclusions—and why you can trust them."

She also dropped the defensiveness.

If a prospective client brought up the $500 startup, she didn't flinch.

"That's a great starting point," she'd say. "But who's on the hook to make it happen?"

The Simplified Offer

Taylor wrestled for days with how to package the shift Drew had suggested. Clients needed clarity, not another complicated menu of services. And the team needed a way to show value without falling back into billable hours or a simple fixed-fee arrangement.

On an early morning jog, the answer came to her: A stepped offer—simple enough to engage, strong enough to protect their value and guarantee the results.

Phase 1: Strategic Forecast—$15K

A structured, expert-guided forecast using the client's data. Clear assumptions, confidence intervals, and full transparency into how the conclusions were reached.

But the forecast wasn't the final product. It was the starting point.

What Phase 1 unlocked:

- A fixed-fee proposal for implementation—based on real data, not guesswork
- A guarantee on outcomes, tied to what the client cared about most
- A trusted partner who had earned their seat at the table

For clients, this first step was small enough to feel safe, but substantial enough to prove commitment. They weren't buying a number—they were testing whether Vic Titious could be trusted with the bigger bet.

Phase 2: Implementation with Outcome Guarantee—$75K–$200K

Tailored implementation based on the forecast: workflow design, change management support, and measurable performance goals.

If the promised results didn't materialize, the client wouldn't pay.

The simplicity surprised people. Some hesitated at the guarantee, others felt relief at finally seeing a clear path forward. But nearly all understood the logic:

Clients weren't paying $15K for a report.

They were securing a path forward—with someone willing to stand behind the results.

Because in the end, they weren't buying forecasts. They were buying confidence that the outcome they cared about would be delivered.

Getting the Board Onboard

For the board, it was not all that easy.

Drew's proposal to pivot again—from selling forecasts to guaranteeing outcomes—wasn't just a pricing tweak. It meant shifting risk from the client to the firm. It meant standing behind every number, with real dollars on the line.

Some board members bristled. *"We can't guarantee the future,"* one protested. "If we miss, it won't just hurt revenue—it will hurt our reputation. No one forgives a broken guarantee." Others worried about cash flow—tying revenue to results could mean long gaps before payment.

But Bailey laid out the case very clearly. Clients were already comparing them to the $500 startup solution. The only way to command trust—and higher fees—was to stand for something different. And GenAI gave them new leverage: the ability to test more scenarios based on the firm's historic data, to monitor outcomes in real time, and to spread risk across projects instead of bearing it client by client.

"Yes, it's riskier than billing by the hour or doing the work for a fixed fee," he admitted. "But it's less risky than becoming irrelevant."

The vote wasn't unanimous. But it passed. Taylor would no longer sell forecasts. She would sell outcomes.

Proving the New Model

Now it was up to Taylor to turn that bold promise into reality.

Two months later, she closed their first true outcome-based client.

It wasn't a test or a discounted pilot.

It was for the full commitment.

A mid-sized manufacturing firm signed the outcome-based agreement:

– $50K up front, with $200K due upon delivery

– Guaranteed 10 percent reduction in inventory costs

– No result, no second payment

The forecast had helped to frame the opportunity.

But this time, the promise wasn't the report.

It was the final outcome.

For the client, the math was obvious. Their annual inventory spend topped $20 million. A 10 percent reduction meant $2 million in savings. Risking $250K against a potential $2 million return was an easy choice—especially with a partner willing to put their fees on the line.

After the client acceptance call, Taylor paced the hallway. Her hands were still shaking when she bumped into Bailey.

"What if we're wrong? What if it doesn't work?", she said.

Bailey smiled. Taylor was starting to sound like

Drew—more nuanced, more realistic, and carrying the weight of accountability as if it were hers alone. He was proud of the transformation she had gone through.

Taylor was ready.

To give her a boost of confidence, he kept his voice calm.

"Then we learn. But we're not guessing. We have the data, the team, and a clear path. We're not betting the firm—we're betting on our ability to deliver. You've got this, Taylor. And you are not alone."

The months that followed were focused and deliberate. The work itself wasn't fundamentally different from what the Corporate Department had done before, which helped. What *had* changed were the business-model constraints Taylor's team now had to operate within. Thanks to the discipline built during the testing phase, they were able to make it work in practice.

Six months later, at the end of a client meeting, the client summed it up simply: *"The cleanest win we've had in years."*

The numbers backed it up. Inventory costs were down 12 percent, surpassing the original 10 percent target. On the spot, the client signed two additional projects with Vic Titious.

The Ripple Effect

That single project marked a turning point.

Over the following nine months:

- Five new clients signed outcome-based agreements
- Several existing clients asked to switch to outcome-based models
- Revenue per client rose by 30 percent
- Client retention improved dramatically

What was even more striking was how the economics began to stack up. One $15K pilot kicked off a new two-phase journey, unlocking a $275K outcome-based engagement—and more than $500K in follow-up work.

At that pace, Taylor, Drew, and Ira could repay the $900K investment in under two years—assuming that their predictions were solid and the profit margins remained the same. Not bad for a firm that only months earlier had been compared to a $500 startup solution.

But success brought its own pressure. Clients wanted more, competitors were watching, and what had started as experimentation was quickly becoming expectation.

Van's solution—combined with the model Vic Titious built on top of it—proved its value. Now the question was whether Vic Titious could scale without stretching the team, the tech, or their credibility too thin.

But for the moment, Taylor let herself enjoy the fruits of her hard work—including a well-earned promotion to lead her own team. "I did it!" Taylor thought. "Or perhaps better—We did it!"—as she recognized that without the help of Drew, Bailey, Ira, and even Van, she would never have been able to pull it all off.

Part 5 Summary

Part 5 traces Vic Titious' transformation—from selling exploratory pilots to offering outcome-based services clients could trust and pay for with confidence.

Initially met with resistance, the team wrestled with how to price, position, and prove the worth of GenAI-powered forecasts. Through trial, reflection, and real client feedback, they realized clients weren't buying forecasts—they were buying results and the confidence to act.

This insight led to a bold shift: from selling time and insight to guaranteeing outcomes with fixed-fee engagements. By embracing transparency, risk-sharing, and a stepped offer model, Taylor and the team turned a $15K pilot into a new revenue stream, sparked wider adoption, and proved the firm could thrive by selling tangible outcomes—not just hours.

Key Takeaways

- Agentic workflows deliver cheap outputs: AI-generated forecasts have minimal standalone value—$500 at best. Automation produces numbers, not insight, ownership, or transformation.
- The real value is what you do with the results:

Forecasts are inputs, not deliverables. Acting on uncertain forecasts with confidence—and standing behind them—became the new value proposition.

- Guaranteeing results changed the game for Vic Titious: By committing to the outcomes generated from the new agentic workflow, Vic Titious took on risk—but unlocked higher-value solutions and deeper client trust.
- Client trust is built through clarity, not complexity: Taylor didn't win trust by making the system more powerful. She earned it by making the logic transparent, challengeable, and actionable.

Reflection Questions

- If your clients compared you to a $500 AI solution tomorrow, what would you stand for?
- Think of a time when your team delivered something valuable—but the client didn't trust it. What was missing?
- Are you more confident offering analysis or guaranteeing impact? Why?
- In your current process, where does human judgment still matter—and is that value visible to others?
- How would your team behave differently if you had to guarantee results instead of billing hours?
- What tools, data, or support would you need

to feel comfortable making those kinds of commitments?

Exercise: Testing a New Business Model

Rewrite one of your current deliverables in outcome-based terms. Instead of "we'll provide insights on X," try: "we'll reduce X by Y percent, or you don't pay." What would it take to make that promise credible?

"The outcome wasn't the grand vision he'd originally envisioned, but by all measures, it was better and bigger."

Conclusion
The Real Work Begins

Bailey's Evolution

Bailey looked back at the transformation with fascination. The outcome wasn't the grand vision he'd originally envisioned, but by all measures, it was better and bigger.

He realized his role wasn't to push big ideas—it was to help people like Taylor and Ira deliver, and guide people like Drew toward new strategic directions.

"I started with a grandiose and misconceived idea about agentic workflows," he reflected. "But the real breakthrough came from focusing on a simple problem: making Drew's team 10 percent more efficient.

In practice, the outcome was much bigger. Taylor's work eliminated a time-consuming loss leader, improved efficiency as a side effect, and created an entirely new revenue stream. Small, disciplined steps produced changes that were both faster and more far-reaching than I ever expected."

He smiled at the thought. "That's what leadership

in innovation really is—celebrating small wins that build momentum, knowing when to challenge and when to support, and creating the conditions for others to succeed. It's certainly not about chasing the biggest vision in the room."

Ira's Growth

The project also transformed Ira. "I used to think my job was to take all the worries away from Drew and her team," she said. "To save them time, shield them from risk, manage the tech, and handle the complexity behind the scenes. I thought that was support."

Looking back, Ira could clearly see the flaw in the accounting project. The team had understood the problem in broad terms, but the work quickly became focused on implementing the vendor's solution. Without a clear, problem-based definition of success, there was no objective way to judge whether things were actually improving.

As a result, the solution was evaluated against an ideal rather than against the status quo. Every imperfection became a reason to hesitate, while the limitations of the existing system faded into the background. Progress was hard to prove, trade-offs were difficult to make, and success quietly became defined by activity rather than outcomes.

The accounting project didn't drag on because the solution was bad. It took years because perfection became the standard—and perfection is an endless target.

Taylor's project worked differently. It was anchored in a clearly defined problem, not in a solution that needed to be perfected. That made trade-offs explicit, progress visible, and the solution adaptable as goals evolved. The work moved forward by learning—not by striving for a flawless implementation.

That contrast forced Ira to confront an uncomfortable truth: her well-intentioned protection and pursuit of perfection had turned her into a bottleneck. With everything running through her, others couldn't prioritize—let alone scale up.

"I was solving too much, too early," she admitted. "And making it too easy for others to stay on the sidelines—partly because I felt my team had to give white-glove services to everyone.

The shift reframed her role. Real partnership meant giving teams like Drew and Taylor the room and the responsibility to solve their challenges—to wrestle with trade-offs, make decisions, and own the outcomes.

"I can help implement solutions," Ira realized. "But I can't deliver results. That's on them."

From that point on, she drew clear lines between support and ownership. Her job was to provide tools, guardrails, and architectural insight—not spoon-feed solutions.

The change didn't just make her more effective. It made her more respected. Teams stopped coming for quick fixes. They came with real questions, clearer intentions, and a willingness to own their part of the process.

And for Ira, that clarity was liberating. She could easily see who was truly committed—and devote her time to where it mattered most. Her team became more productive, and she was happier in her role than she had ever been.

Taylor's Transformation

Taylor's growth was the most dramatic.

She had started the project feeling tentative—more concerned about how GenAI might replace her than how it could elevate her. As she got more comfortable using GenAI, her fear gave way to curiosity. Then confidence. Instead of seeing the tools as a threat, she began to see GenAI as leverage—amplifying what she was good at and freeing her to focus on the bigger picture.

And yet, if the firm had not come around, she probably would have walked away. Fortunately, that didn't happen.

The project didn't just teach her AI. It thrust her into leadership—fast.

She wasn't just sitting in meetings anymore; she was driving them. Managing timelines. Engaging clients. Navigating resistance. Pitching new ideas internally.

"No book or course could've prepared me for all of this," she said. "You learn to manage stakeholders or pitch a new model by doing—when there's a real deadline, real pressure, and real consequences."

On occasion, it had felt like being thrown into the deep end. But knowing Drew, Ira, and Bailey wouldn't let her drown gave her the courage to try and the opportunity to learn at incredible speed. As a result, she had managed to not just survive but thrive.

And thrive she did. By the end of the project, Taylor had helped launch a new division for Vic Titious—more productized than their traditional offerings, built on an outcome-guaranteed business model, and growing fast.

She wasn't just implementing solutions anymore. She had redesigned Vic Titious' business model.

"The pressure was intense," she admitted. "But it forced me to think differently—about value, risk, and what clients truly care about. I learned more in these last eighteen months than in the previous four years."

She hadn't just kept up with the future. She helped shape it—and found her place in it.

Van's Realization

"I always thought my job was pretty simple," Van said. "Get the deal done. Get the signature. That's when things either move or they don't."

He paused, then shrugged. "What happens after that? I used to tell myself that was adoption, customer care, and change management. Someone else's problem."

Working with Taylor made that line of thinking harder to defend.

"Watching her wrestle from intent to disruption to something that actually worked… that stretch in the middle?" He shook his head. "I never really paid attention to it before. But that's clearly where things fall apart."

Selling, he realized, wasn't the hard part. "Getting people to actually use their software—that was harder. And getting them to see the return they were promised at the start? That's where it would get uncomfortable."

In the past, he'd leaned on a familiar pattern. "As long as we had one or two champions, we were fine. Just one person was often enough to keep the renewal alive." He smiled, then hesitated. "I took renewals as proof that we were doing well."

Now he wasn't so sure.

"Turns out that's a pretty thin safety net," he said. "It keeps the contract afloat, but it doesn't mean the client is getting real value."

Working with Vic Titious showed him another way. "It was slower. Messier. And honestly, more work. But staying with the team long enough to help them turn a tool into something that actually changed how they worked—that was invaluable."

He thought for a moment. "I didn't just sell them something. We built it together. And that changed the relationship."

And if there was one thing he'd learned from Taylor, it was this: honesty outlasts bluff. It wasn't just more sustainable—it was the foundation for trust.

The collaboration and trust gave him something no

sales deck ever could: a story of real transformation he could share with future clients—and a relationship that would lead to renewals, expansions, and referrals for years to come.

The only thing he wished now was that his own firm measured success the same way his clients did—not in contracts signed, but in value created.

Drew's Closing Reflection

"For a long time, I thought GenAI would be incremental," Drew said. "Another upgrade. Something Ira would manage and Taylor would explore."

She paused. "I didn't really understand it until I had to use it myself. That's when it stopped being abstract. Only then did I see how much it could reshape how work flowed, what clients expected, and what they valued."

When she spoke about Taylor, pride came easily. "What she pulled off shouldn't be underestimated. The energy, the stamina, the guts to keep going when things got uncomfortable. That takes something."

She didn't say it outright, but the pride carried a sting.

Twice now, Drew had handed clients to Taylor's team to keep them from defecting to the startup. It was the right decision—there was no question about that. Still, each time it happened, it left her with a quiet awareness she couldn't shake. Her own portfolio was becoming dependable rather than distinctive. The work still paid the bills, but they no longer fed her ambition. Watching

Taylor build something new stirred a mix of possibility and—if she was honest—a twinge of envy.

"I coached her to pass me," Drew said. "And she did."

She let that sit, realizing that somewhere along the way she had moved from first chair to second—still vital, still needed, but no longer leading the melody.

For a long time, she'd hoped that wouldn't matter—that past experience and success would be enough to secure her standing in the firm. That she could stay on top by making small tweaks to what already existed. Change without having to start over. "I think I wanted transformation that didn't ask too much of me—innovation from the couch, never too uncomfortable," she admitted. "Which, in hindsight, feels naïve."

The sustainability initiative came back to her then. "That had a mission everyone believed in. We launched it with real enthusiasm." She shook her head. "But we never tied it to the firm's business goals. So when pressure hit—when something more urgent came along—it slipped. Not because people didn't care, but because it seemed optional."

"Taylor's project wasn't optional. The business goal was clear from the start. When trade-offs came up, we couldn't dodge them. We had to choose." She smiled faintly. "That makes a difference."

Drew leaned back. "I've been thinking a lot about what comes next. And honestly, I don't know yet."

What she did know was that staying relevant wouldn't

mean standing at a distance. It would mean getting back into the frontline—hands-on, not secondhand. Accepting that what clients valued, and what counted as expertise, had already shifted.

It had crossed her mind that perhaps she could coach more Taylors. Shape the next generation instead of leading from the front. But the thought vanished almost as soon as it appeared. Her department no longer attracted talent like that—and if she was honest, Bailey and the board wouldn't give her the same benefit of the doubt now that she was playing second chair.

That realization cut deep. Influence wasn't something you earned once and kept forever. If she wanted to matter, she couldn't just mentor from the sidelines. She had been bold once—had taken risks when the outcome wasn't clear. The question was whether she could do that again, with more miles on the odometer and more weight to carry.

She also gave herself some grace. She had taken Taylor's vigor for granted—her drive, her stamina, her relentless follow-through. Now she saw the weight Taylor had carried, and the courage it had required. Respect replaced the sting.

The future, she realized, wouldn't be about reclaiming the top spot. It would be about choosing the right hill to climb—celebrating Taylor's ascent while finding a slope of her own.

Maybe re-energizing the sustainability initiative was that hill, this time anchored in real outcomes instead of good intentions. Maybe it was something else entirely.

But first, Drew decided, she would take a real vacation. Time away from day-to-day decisions. Time to let the noise settle, to see the landscape more clearly, and to decide what came next.

First chair or second, she wasn't done playing.

The Broader Implications

Drew wasn't alone in her reckoning. Her questions—about relevance, risk, and reinvention—echoed across the firm. What started as one team's experiment had become a blueprint for change. And with that change came lessons no one could ignore—lessons about what GenAI really meant for Vic Titious.

Their success highlights several key insights about GenAI implementation:

1. Trust is the Real Barrier

Technical capability matters far less than confidence in the outcomes. With GenAI, outputs are probabilistic, directional, and most often useful, but never flawless.

For **clients**, that uncertainty feels risky: numbers can hide assumptions, answers can mask blind spots or be blatantly wrong. For **users**, it creates hesitation: if they don't trust the process, they likely stall instead of act.

That's why adoption hinges on trust, not features. Without trust, agentic workflows collapse into hesitation.

With trust, they can deliver impact and create momentum for change.

2. Start Small, Think Big

It is easier to make something big out of something small that has traction than to start big and try to gain traction.

3. Focus on Outcomes, Not Tools

Clients don't want GenAI—they want results. Frame solutions around business outcomes, not technical capabilities.

4. Change the Business Model

GenAI's real power often comes from enabling new ways of working, not just making old ways better or faster.

The Next Chapter

As the story closes, Vic Titious is no longer just experimenting with GenAI—it's scaling its success.

What began as a narrowly defined efficiency pilot project evolved into something much larger. The Agentic Workflow Project Drew and Taylor championed is now the blueprint for a new way of working and serving clients: more collaborative, more transparent, and outcome-focused.

The firm is preparing to expand this model into other departments and practice areas—taking what they learned in one corner of the business and applying it more broadly. GenAI isn't about shiny technology anymore. It's about how they work.

Bailey's upcoming board presentation looks nothing like the one he gave six months earlier.

Back then, he was asking for $900K to explore a vision—armed mostly with market trends, internal urgency, and a few promising anecdotes.

This time, about fifteen months later, he walks in with results:

- A 30 percent increase in revenue per client in the pilot group
- Fifteen new clients acquired in sectors they previously struggled to reach
- Measurable improvements in client retention
- And an ROI on the full investment—paid by the profits of the new offering.

He clicks to the final slide.

It's not a hockey stick chart. It's a simple timeline—marked with steady milestones, each one backed by evidence.

"Sometimes the best way to get a big idea approved," he tells the board, "is to prove it works at a small scale first."

He pauses, letting that land.

"That's how we'll operate the Agentic Workflow

Investment Fund going forward," Bailey said. "Structured, milestone-based investments. No big bets without small wins first. Funding tied to demonstrated outcomes—learning early, scaling only when the evidence supports it. And when initiatives deliver, those results will help replenish the fund."

There's a moment of silence.

Then, one by one, heads begin to nod.

The board approves his ask for a $1 million Agentic Workflow Investment Fund—unanimously.

And for the first time in a long while, Vic Titious isn't just adapting to change.

They're defining it.

How It Feels to Work The RISE Way

The Friday after the board meeting, Bailey sat alone with the last few slides—not to prepare, just to absorb.

"At first," he thought, "agentic workflows felt like a tool for innovation teams—something we'd use here and there." He leaned back. "Now I see them as a leadership model. The approach taught us to take ownership—not just of effort, but of outcomes."

It wasn't just the results. It was how people were showing up.

In a conference room down the hall, Taylor wrapped up a planning session with her team. The conversation had shifted from timelines to targets—and what it would take to deliver on a new client commitment.

Afterward, a junior associate asked how she felt about making such a bold budget ask.

"Back then, asking for $50K terrified me," Taylor said. "I agonized over every slide. Every word. Now?" She shrugged. "I know what I'm asking for. I know what I'm committing to. And I know what I need to do to deliver it. That's what makes it a deal—not a plea."

From another vantage point, Ira noticed the same shift. In the early days, she'd tried to sit at the center—double-checking options, running backup scenarios, shielding people from risk. Over coffee with Drew, she admitted: "I used to think my job was to take risk off each team's plate. Now I realize my job is to support the people willing to take risks—smartly, with structure, and with skin in the game."

Drew nodded. "You've certainly opened my eyes to what's possible."

And at the firm level, those moments added up. The RISE way wasn't a slogan; it became a cadence:

- **Return:** Teams tied every initiative to a concrete outcome and reviewed it weekly—what we promised, what we delivered, what changed.
- **Invest:** Funding moved through small gates—evidence first, bigger bets next. No big checks without small wins.
- **Support:** Enablement replaced handholding. Tools, playbooks, office hours—yes. Leaving it to chance, spoon-feeding—no.
- **Expectations:** Every project began with a

one-page commitment charter: target, timeline, owners, hours, and success metrics.

That's how it felt to work the RISE way: clearer, more accountable, and more human.

The Uncomfortable Truth About GenAI

This book began with a simple premise: GenAI will change how professional services work. What the story reveals is more unsettling—and more profound.

GenAI doesn't just automate tasks. It alters the economics of expertise. It reshapes how value is created, who gets to deliver it, and what clients are actually willing to pay for.

The technical capabilities—automated analysis, faster forecasting, streamlined workflows—were all achievable. But they weren't enough. The real breakthrough came when the team realized those capabilities didn't matter unless they changed too: how they worked, how they led, and how they defined value.

The Paradox of Agentic Workflows

The irony of agentic workflows is that they're not really about workflows. They're about agency. The power to let go. The confidence to make commitments and stand behind them. The support to deliver expected results.

The clarity to know when it is a success—and the courage to admit when it isn't.

That's not a technical problem. That's a leadership

challenge.

GenAI can generate forecasts, automate analysis, streamline processes, and a lot more. However, AI can't take responsibility. It can't build trust. It can't make the kind of commitments that create lasting client relationships.

Only humans can do that.

And that's the opportunity.

A New Kind of Leadership

The RISE framework—**Return, Invest, Support, Expectations**—began as a structure for engaging people in projects, rather than for investing and managing these projects. Over time, it became something even bigger: A model for leadership.

- **Return**: Leaders who connect outcomes *with* activity create the conditions for real accountability. It's not just about goals or being busy—it's about ensuring commitment drives results.
- **Invest**: When people have skin in the game—time, reputation, relationships—they show up differently. They stop waiting for direction and start owning what happens next. It also means investing in GenAI proficiency—so people understand how these tools work and know when to trust the outcomes.
- **Support**: The most powerful support isn't about removing risk. It's about equipping others to take ownership—with structure, scaffolding, and space

to grow—so risks are reduced through clarity and confidence. Whether it is a course to upskill or a gentle push to do those client interviews, we all have things we hesitate to do because we aren't really sure how to go about them.

- **Expectations**: Clear commitments don't limit learning—they make it possible. When everyone knows what success looks like, failure becomes feedback instead of a crisis.

RISE didn't just change how Vic Titious managed projects. It changed how they led at every level.

Beyond the First Success

Twelve months after Bailey's unanimous board approval for the Agentic Workflow Investment Fund, Vic Titious looked like a different company. Revenue per client increased company-wide. Client retention was at an all-time high. The outcome-based model was expanding into new practice areas.

But the real transformation wasn't in the numbers.

You could hear it in the hallway conversations.

Drew and a partner in Mergers & Acquisitions weren't discussing hours anymore—they were sketching a pricing model tied to case resolution speed.

Taylor was mentoring a junior associate—not on how to write better memos, but how to frame an initiative so it could earn funding from the Agentic Workflow Fund.

Ira had started hosting internal roundtables—not

to gatekeep ideas, but to help teams pressure-test their assumptions before pitching the next iteration of their offering.

In pockets all across the firm, something unexpected was happening:

People were talking about what was possible.

Not just of projects.

Of problems. Of progress. Of client value.

They weren't just executing initiatives.

They were designing how the firm would grow next.

What Actually Changed

The transformation wasn't just in performance metrics. It was in behavior and belief.

GenAI found its real place. Not a magic bullet. Not a gimmick. A useful tool. A thinking partner. A spark. A productivity booster for the right tasks. People understood its value and its limits.

People stopped waiting for permission. They started making commitments: clear, measurable, accountable. They didn't ask, "Can I do this?" Rather, "What will it take to deliver this?"

Time stopped being the product. Outcomes became the offer. Forecasts turned into guarantees. Reports became routes to results.

RISE moved from framework to culture. You could see it in the seams of the firm:

- Project reviews focused on what was learned

and achieved, not projections of what might be possible.

- Budgets flowed to teams that did the hard work: testing assumptions and de-risking their projects.
- Ownership was backed by structure and guidance, rather than expecting people to figure things out on their own.
- Plans opened with explicit expectations—and closed with evidence and lessons learned.

In the end, agentic workflows weren't just a tool. They became a way of learning and leading—anchored in outcomes, trust, and shared accountability.

The Reality Check

Let's be honest about what this book doesn't address.

Real organizations aren't as neat as Vic Titious. People have complicated motivations, competing priorities, and political pressures that don't resolve cleanly in a few months.

Bailey, Drew, Ira, Van, and Taylor are composites—simplified versions of the complex colleagues you work with every day.

People get sick, have family emergencies, struggle with confidence, resist change, and sometimes just have bad days.

The business case that worked so cleanly in this

story might take years to prove in reality. The board that approved expansion funding unanimously might, in your organization, require months of negotiation and compromise.

That's the real work.

This book provided the framework. But implementation requires the messy, patient, persistent work of changing how people think, feel, and act.

And that's on you.

Your Next Chapter Starts Now

The question isn't whether GenAI will change your industry. It already has.

The question is whether you'll use it to do the same work faster—or to do fundamentally different work better.

Don't wait for a perfect plan—or a $900K budget. Start with:

- **One real problem** worth solving
- (At least) **One person who is** willing to take ownership
- **One commitment** you can deliver on
- **One success** that proves the model works

Start small. Build evidence. Expand methodically. Make it real.

The Real ROI

The return on investment from agentic workflows isn't just measured in efficiency gains or cost savings.

It's measured in confidence.

The confidence to make commitments instead of excuses. The confidence to guarantee results instead of billing hours. The confidence to lead change instead of waiting for it.

When you can clearly articulate:

- **What return** will you deliver
- **What are you willing to invest** to make it happen
- **What support** you need to succeed
- **What expectations** are you committing to meet

You're not just implementing a workflow. You're leading a transformation.

The future belongs to those who can bridge the gap between where technology can take over and what humans are uniquely positioned to do. The tools are ready. The question is: Are you?

Key Takeaways

1. **Board Dynamics**: In professional service firms, innovation investments require proof of demand before approval. Start small and build evidence.
2. **Trust Building**: GenAI solutions fail without trust. Show your work, explain limitations, and demonstrate results transparently.
3. **Business Model Innovation**: The biggest opportunities often come from changing how you

deliver value, not just what you deliver.

4. **Character Growth**: Real transformation happens when people are challenged to grow beyond their comfort zones while being supported to succeed.
5. **Sustainable Change**: Momentum comes from small wins, not grand gestures that fizzle out.

Reflection Questions

- How does your organization handle AI investments? What evidence do decision-makers need to see?
- When introducing new GenAI tools or agentic workflows, how do you build trust with skeptical users?
- What aspects of your business model could change if you guaranteed outcomes instead of selling time?
- How do you balance supporting team members while ensuring they have "skin in the game"?

References

Afeyan, Noubar, and Gary P. Pisano. "What Evolution Can Teach Us About Innovation." Harvard Business Review 99, no. 5 (September–October 2021): 62–72. https://hbr.org/2021/09/what-evolution-can-teach-us-about-innovation.

Amabile, Teresa M., and Steven Kramer. The Progress Principle: Using Small Wins to Ignite Joy, Engagement, and Creativity at Work. Boston: Harvard Business Review Press, 2011.

Ancona, Deborah. "Outward Bound: Strategies for Team Survival in an Organization." Administrative Science Quarterly 35, no. 4 (December 1990): 634–665. https://doi.org/10.2307/2393515.

Blindenbach-Driessen, Floor, and Jan van den Ende. "Opportunistic New Product Development." In The PDMA Handbook of Innovation and New Product Development, 4th ed., edited by Abbie Griffin, Charles H. Noble, and Serdar S. Durmusoglu, 227–246. Hoboken, NJ: Wiley, 2023.

Blindenbach-Driessen, Floor, and Jan van den Ende. 2014. "The Locus of Innovation: The Effect of a Separate Innovation Unit on Exploration, Exploitation, and Ambidexterity in Manufacturing and Service Firms." Journal of Product Innovation Management.

Blindenbach-Driessen, Floor, and Jan van den Ende. 2010. "Innovation Management Practices Compared: The Example of Project-Based Firms." Journal of Product Innovation Management 27 (5): 705–724.

Dawson, Angus, and Katy George. "New Rules for Teamwork." Harvard Business Review, September–October 2024. https://hbr.org/2024/09/new-rules-for-teamwork.

Dell'Acqua, Fabrizio, Edward McFowland III, Ethan Mollick, Hila Lifshitz-Assaf, Katherine C. Kellogg, Saran Rajendran, Lisa Krayer, François Candelon, and Karim R. Lakhani. Navigating the Jagged Technological Frontier: Field Experimental Evidence of the Effects of AI on Knowledge Worker Productivity and Quality. Working

Paper 24-013. Boston: Harvard Business School, 2023. https://www.hbs.edu/ris/Publication%20Files/24-013_d9b45b68-9e74-42d6-a1c6-c72fb70c7282.pdf.

Dew, Nicholas, Saras D. Sarasvathy, Stuart Read, and Robert Wiltbank. "Affordable Loss: Behavioral Economic Aspects of the Plunge Decision." Strategic Entrepreneurship Journal 3, no. 2 (2009): 105–126. https://doi.org/10.1002/sej.66.

Dziri, Nouha, Zineb Mouna, Zineb Kouta, Ali El-Ghamidi, and Nizar Habash. "LLMs Will Always Hallucinate, and We Need to Live with This." In Natural Language Understanding and Processing, Vol. 1, edited by Ayoub Bounhas, Rachid Benlamri, Abdelkrim Mezghiche, and Azzeddine Zine, 631–653. Lecture Notes in Networks and Systems 999. Cham: Springer Nature Switzerland, 2025.

Edmondson, Amy. Right Kind of Wrong: The Science of Failing Well. New York: Atria Books, 2023.

El-Gazzar, Armin. "The Probabilistic Paradox: Why LLMs Fail in Deterministic Domains—and How to Fix It." Medium, April 4, 2024. https://medium.com/@ensigno/the-probabilistic-paradox-why-llms-fail-in-deterministic-domains-and-how-to-fix-it-be21b5e20bda.

Ford, Paul. "The A.I. Disruption We've Been Waiting for Has Arrived." The New York Times, February 18, 2026. https://www.nytimes.com/2026/02/18/opinion/ai-software.html.

Gardner, Heidi K., and Ivan A. Matviak. Smarter Collaboration: A New Approach to Breaking Down Barriers and Transforming Work. Boston: Harvard Business Review Press, 2022.

"Johannes Gutenberg." Encyclopaedia Britannica. Last modified June 21, 2025. https://www.britannica.com/biography/Johannes-Gutenberg.

Kijkuit, Bob, and Jan van den Ende. "The Organizational Life of an Idea: Integrating Social Network, Creativity and Decision-Making Perspectives." Journal of Management Studies 44, no. 6 (September 2007): 863–882. https://doi.org/10.1111/j.1467-6486.2007.00711.x.

Klein, Gary. "Performing a Project Premortem." Harvard Business Review, September 2007. https://hbr.org/2007/09/performing-a-project-premortem.

Kotter, John P. Leading Change. Boston: Harvard Business School Press, 1996.

Mankins, Michael. "Lean Strategy Making." Harvard Business Review, May–June 2025. https://hbr.org/2025/05/lean-strategy-making.

Markel, Howard. "In 1850, Ignaz Semmelweis Saved Lives with Three Words: Wash Your Hands." PBS NewsHour, May 15, 2015. https://www.pbs.org/newshour/health/ignaz-semmelweis-doctor-prescribed-hand-washing.

Markus, M. Lynne, and Claudia Loebbecke. "Commoditized Digital Processes and Business Community Platforms: New Opportunities and Challenges for Digital Business Strategies." MIS Quarterly 37, no. 2 (June 2013): 649–653. https://www.jstor.org/stable/pdf/43825930.pdf.

McGrath, Rita Gunther, and Ian C. MacMillan. Discovery-Driven Growth: A Breakthrough Process to Reduce Risk and Seize Opportunity. Boston: Harvard Business Press, 2009.

Mintzberg, Henry. "Structure in 5's: A Synthesis of the Research on Organization Design." Management Science 26, no. 3 (March 1980): 322–341. https://www.jstor.org/stable/2630506.

MIT Sloan School of Management. Workforce Intelligence: From MIT Experts, Strategies to Transform Skills, Roles, and Human Potential across Your Organization. Cambridge: MIT Sloan School of Management, 2025. https://mitsloan.mit.edu.

MIT NANDA. The GenAI Divide: State of AI in Business 2025. Cambridge, MA: MIT Media Lab, 2025.

Mollick, Ethan. Co-Intelligence: Living and Working with AI. New York: Portfolio, 2024.

Ramanathan, Tara. "Watt Steam Engine." Encyclopaedia Britannica. Last modified June 21, 2025. https://www.britannica.com/technology/Watt-steam-engine.

Riedl, Christoph, Hila Lifshitz-Assaf, and Michael Tushman. "Do You See What I See? How Expertise and a Decision-Maker Role Influence the Recognition and Selection of Novel Ideas." Research Policy 42, no. 10 (2013): 1973–1987. https://doi.org/10.1016/j.respol.2013.06.005.

Riedl, Christoph, and Ben Weidmann. "Quantifying AI-Human Synergy." Seventh Annual Conference on Learning for Language (CoLLas 2025). OpenReview, 2025. https://openreview.net/pdf?id=Yhqa8Ljzrj.

Stanford Institute for Human-Centered Artificial Intelligence. AI Index Report. Stanford University, 2025. https://aiindex.stanford.edu.

Tidd, Joe, and John R. Bessant. Managing Innovation: Integrating Technological, Market, and Organizational Change. 7th ed. Hoboken, NJ: John Wiley & Sons, 2020.

Young, Alistair, and Tony Murphy. Managing IT Vendors: Getting the Best from Suppliers and Partners. Cambridgeshire: IT Governance Publishing, 2019.

Thank You

Books don't come into being on their own—and *Rise Above AI Chaos* is no exception. This book is the result of countless conversations, reflections, and moments of encouragement. I owe deep gratitude to the many people who walked beside me along the way.

First and foremost, to my beloved husband, Wim. Lieve Wim, you have walked with me through the deepest valleys and encouraged me to climb the highest mountains, including this one. There are no words adequate to describe my gratitude for your unwavering love and support.

To my children, who each helped shape the character of Taylor and whose drive, hard work, honesty, and insight found their way into these pages.

To my parents, for their unconditional support and love—no matter what I do or how far away I am—and for instilling in me the curiosity, perseverance, and confidence to take on any challenge. To Aalke, who showed me early on that a healthy work–life balance is possible—a lesson I carry still. And to my brother, sister, and in-laws—for always being there, and for your honest feedback, examples, and encouragement.

To Martha and Trish, who inspired me to start writing this book in the first place—you gave me the push I needed to begin.

To my clients, whose determination to deliver results has continually reinforced why this work matters—your efforts and achievements are reflected throughout these pages. And to Tom Freiling and his team, whose enthusiasm for the concept and editorial expertise carried this project across the finish line.

In naming a few, I risk leaving many unnamed. Please know—family, mentors, friends, colleagues, and neighbors—all of you have contributed in one way or another. Your presence, ideas, and encouragement are woven throughout these pages.

Finally, to you, the reader—thank you for choosing to rise above the noise and explore how we can lead with purpose in the age of AI. May these pages spark clarity, courage, and confidence on your own journey.

About the Author

Floor Blindenbach Driessen, PhD, is the founder of Organizing4Innovation, where she helps law firms and other professional service organizations rise above AI chaos and turn technology into measurable results. She has reinvented her career many times—crossing the Atlantic three times and shifting from chemical engineer to academic researcher, assistant professor, healthcare innovation leader, and now advisor to firms navigating AI and digital transformation.

She has seen firsthand the disruptive power of GenAI. For six years, she poured her soul, earnings, and expertise into building an innovation tool—only to watch GenAI outcompete it overnight. Even with deep knowledge of innovation management, she came face-to-face with a hard truth: no one is immune to disruption.

If there's one thing she's learned along the way, it's this: **Tools don't create change. People do.** Whether it's new technology, redesigns of workflows, or organizational change, Floor focuses on the human side of innovation—building momentum, reducing friction, and making ROI tangible.

She brings more than twenty-five years of experience

and holds a PhD in management from Erasmus University Rotterdam. Floor lives in Williamsburg, VA and Albany, NY with her husband. Their three children are now thriving young adults.

More information about her work can be found at: organizing4innovation.com.

www.ingramcontent.com/pod-product-compliance
Lightning Source LLC
LaVergne TN
LVHW091134080826
845145LV00008B/2148

* 9 7 8 1 9 6 3 7 0 1 9 6 8 *